MW01194423

SECRETS TO WINNING GOVERNMENT CONTRACTS

How any small business owner
can become a profitable
PRIME FEDERAL CONTRACTOR
in 12 months or less

Also by Martin Saenz

#1 Amazon Bestseller

Note Investing Made Easier

How to Buy and Profit from Distressed Mortgages

Available in Paperback, Kindle and Audiobook
On Amazon and Audible.com

Contact Martin Saenz

on the web
https://www.govcon.win/

by email

info@govcon.win

SECRETS TO WINNING GOVERNMENT CONTRACTS

How any small business owner
can become a profitable
PRIME FEDERAL CONTRACTOR
in 12 months or less

MARTIN SAENZ MBA MS

POWER
HOUSE
PUBLISHING

ALEXANDRIA
VIRGINIA

Secrets To Winning Government Contracts

How any small business owner can become
a profitable prime federal contractor
in 12 months or less

by Martin Saenz

Published by:
Powerhouse Publishing
625 N. Washington Street, Suite 425
Alexandria, Virginia 22314

info@powerhousepublishing.net
703-982-0984

ISBN First Paperback Edition: 1986408043

First paperback printing March 2018
Printed in the United States of America

Saenz, Martin
Secrets to winning government contracts, how any small business owner can become a profitable prime federal contractor in 12 months or less

1st paperback ed.

ISBN-13: 978-1986408042
ISBN-10: 1986408043

Dedication

This book is dedicated to my wife, Ruth. She believed in me and had vision when we were starting out flat broke on the bottom of the learning curve. That is why we are Team Saenz for life. And to my four beautiful children, Joshua, Zachary, Emily, and Elijah. May I always be there to help you develop and grow in life.

Acknowledgements

I would like to express my gratitude to some of the folks whose professional advice and encouragement led to my growth and success in the government contracting space and inspired me to write this book.

I have to start with the Community Business Partnership in Springfield Virginia whose mission is to offer educational and support services to the community. We found the most caring and loving people there who helped Ruth and I learn to be business owners. They go above and beyond the call of duty with all the courses they offer and time they donate to folks starting out. Kathy Wheeler, Sheina Waddell, Barbara Wrigley, I'm talking to you.

Tracey Jeter and LaVerne Greene with the now Capital Region Minority Supplier Development Council. You gave guidance over our early years and helped bring us into the fold with larger corporations. The work you do has lasting effects on small MBE businesses and I have to say Thank You. LaVerne came to our home to conduct the certification interview and saw something bigger for ourselves than we saw at the time.

And to Harry Ponack, a 30+ year veteran in selling to the Federal Government. Your help and partnership has been valuable to me from my beginning days. May we collaborate on many business initiatives going forward.

I have to acknowledge my wife, Ruth, who ran the company with me side by side for many years. She always stayed in the background and made sure that quality control and efficiency was in place with each project. I couldn't have done any of this without you.

Disclaimer

Achieving success as a prime contractor to the federal government requires a significant investment of money, time and dedication over the course of months and years. Simply reading this book will not ensure your success

The content provided in this book is for informational purposes only. It should not be considered legal or financial advice. You should consult with an attorney or other professional to determine what may be best for your individual needs.

Neither Martin Saenz nor Powerhouse Publishing make any guarantee or other promise as to any results that may be obtained from using the information in this book. No one should make any business decision without first consulting his or her own financial advisor, attorney, CPA, etc. and conducting his or her own research and due diligence. To the maximum extent permitted by law, the author and publisher disclaim any and all liability in the event any information, commentary, analysis, opinions, advice and/or recommendations prove to be inaccurate, incomplete or unreliable, or result in any investment or other losses.

About the Author

Martin Saenz holds a Master of Business Administration from Drexel University and a Master of Science in Project Management from George Washington University.

In 2004 he was fired from a corporate job he hated and, along with his wife Ruth, founded a government contracting company in the basement of their home.

Starting with almost no capital, they bought equipment and paid expenses using credit cards, running up tens of thousands of dollars in debt before their company began to earn a profit.

Over the course of 14 years and scores of successfully-completed prime federal contracts, Martin and Ruth have built a multimillion-dollar company that now operates out of its own large warehouse and production facility in Northern Virginia, outside of Washington, DC.

During that time, Martin, Ruth and their team have confronted and overcome every conceivable obstacle, including three shutdowns of the entire federal government!

Secrets to Winning Government Contracts is a complete How To guide for any small business owner who wants to begin selling to the world's largest buyer of goods and services: The United States Federal Government.

Table of Contents

Foreword

This book has been a revelation to me.

For over 40 years, I have been providing marketing support, training and services in the Washington, DC area. Naturally, many business owners along the way have asked me if I could help them market their products or services to the federal government.

Up until this point, my answer has always been the same, "Absolutely not. Selling to the government is a complete mystery to me." As a marketing professional, having to reply in this fashion has always been a bit embarrassing. But, as Dirty Harry once famously opined, "A man's got to know his limitations."

Thanks to Martin Saenz and *Secrets To Winning Government Contracts*, my answer to that question today, and from this point forward, is completely different.

In this book, Martin illuminates many dark corners of the federal contracting process and makes clear that government buyers, just like buyers in every other market, are human beings with human objectives, needs and fears. That was my first revelation; that federal buyers could be reached at an emotional level in spite of layers bureaucracy and acquisition regulations.

My next revelation came in Chapter 4, Competitive Intelligence. There Martin explains that there is detailed information, available online at no charge, which will tell you everything you could want to know about which agency bought which product or service from which contractor, when, and for how much. In the commercial world, companies resort to espionage to gather that type of intel. But Uncle Sam makes it available to anyone for free on an ongoing basis. Who knew?

This book delivers those gems along with many other AH HAH moments. I won't attempt to synopsize them all here, but there are a couple more important points I would like to leave you with. The first thing you need to understand is that Martin and Ruth Saenz started their exhibit fabrication business in their basement, and built it into a multimillion-dollar prime federal contracting company, operating out of a large production and warehouse facility which they own. What you will read in these pages is the real deal, not theory about what might work.

Secondly, Martin Saenz is not only an experienced federal contractor, but also a generous, empathetic and engaged teacher, who shares with you everything you need to know to get started replicating his success selling your product or service to the world's largest buyer, the United States Government.

Don't wait. Start reading and start doing.

Frank Felker
President
Digital Media Positioning

Chapter 1

Introduction

Welcome to *Secrets to Winning Government Contracts*! Before we get started, I want to tell you a little about my background, how my wife Ruth and I came to launch a federal contracting business and how it has worked out for us. I also want to explain how the information in this book was structured and what you're going to learn.

After receiving my undergraduate degree in my early twenties, I turned my attention to checking all the right boxes and doing all the things we are told to do to have a stable, rewarding, long-term career in corporate America. I earned an MBA and another master's degree in project management; I got a regular job and started investing in my 401k. But I quickly found that this stereotypical lifestyle wasn't for me. In 2004, after numerous disagreements with my corporate "superiors," I was fired.

That unpleasant experience ended up being one of the best things that could have ever happened to me. My wife and I began exploring options that were out of the box and wouldn't tie us down to a typical "J-O-B." We decided to form a signage and museum exhibit company that had the sole focus of selling to the federal government.

It wasn't easy. We launched in 2005 with few resources and no assets. We took on hundreds of thousands of dollars in debt to get started and ran our business out of our basement. We experienced all the pains of startup; making payroll the day of, stretching out vendor payments to the maximum extent possible – everything that thousands of entrepreneurs across the nation have experienced.

One thing we intentionally avoided was the low-hanging fruit of commercial work. There was plenty of it out there, but we knew that engaging with it would distract us from our long-term goal of working exclusively with the federal government. Small contracts with corporate accounts would have kept us so wrapped up in the day-to-day existence of hopping from one job to the next that we wouldn't have had time to invest in our long-term future.

Eventually we gained traction as federal contractors and never looked back. By 2009 our business had grown from a debt-encumbered small operation in a basement to a multimillion dollar corporation that had to purchase commercial space in order to meet our production and storage requirements. We had prime contracts with the Pentagon, USDA, Smithsonian, Department of Defense, National

Defense University, and the Department of State. The company has continued to develop and increase in size ever since.

This book is for the small guy or gal working out of their home or a small office who has the ambition and determination to become a successful federal contractor. I'm going to teach you how to sell directly to the federal government as a prime contractor, without going through a middle man. This isn't easy but is certainly worth the work required. The federal government is the biggest buyer in the world. Our learning curve took three years of hard effort before we began consistently landing contracts. I've taken those lessons and coalesced them into the book you're now holding.

Book Structure

This book is divided into four sections:

- Section 1 – Goal Setting
  - Chapter 1: Introduction
  - Chapter 2: Strategy Overview
  - Chapter 3: Core Competency
  - Chapter 4: Competitive Intelligence
- Section 2 – Massive Action Plan (MAP)
  - Chapter 5: What is a MAP?
  - Chapter 6: Profile and Reputation
  - Chapter 7: Associations & Social Media
  - Chapter 8: Small Business Events

- ○ Chapter 9: Building your Pipeline
- • Section 3 – Getting Setup to Bid
  - ○ Chapter 10: Procurement Forecast
  - ○ Chapter 11: Procurement Websites
  - ○ Chapter 12: Capabilities Statement
  - ○ Chapter 13: Proposal Generating Systems
  - ○ Chapter 14: End of Fiscal Year
- • Section 4 – Designations and Teaming
  - ○ Chapter 15: Looking to Team?
  - ○ Chapter 16: Small Business Designations

The first step is Goal Setting. This is a typical starting point for any project, but there are some unique steps to take when bidding on federal projects. Next, I'll teach you how to create a MAP, a Massive Action Plan. Procuring prime contracts with the federal government is a long-term process with a lot of puzzle pieces to put together. Having a defined, strategic structure in place is essential to consistently winning government contracts.

The third step is Getting Set Up to Bid. Here I'll teach you how to source the bids, called *requests for proposals*, or RFPs. In the last section of the book I'll discuss Designations and Teaming. There are specific vehicles the federal government has set up that will give you an advantage in bidding, if you qualify. Examples of these are GSA schedules, Small Business Certification from the Small Business Administration (SBA), HUB Zone, and various minority classifications such as a veteran-owned or woman-owned small business. The important thing to remember here is that, while these designations give you an advantage, they don't magically create your ability to do business. At the end of the day you must have the expertise and resources to fully perform on every contract you receive.

One of the most important things to remember is that you don't know everything. Seeking professional advice in a variety of areas, e.g., legal counsel, a certified public accountant (CPA), and financial planners is vital to your success. You want to make sure that your contracts are built on a solid foundation and getting help in areas where you're weak is key to this process.

Case Study Contributor

In order to make this book as relevant as possible to business owners who have little to no experience contracting with the federal government, I have been mentoring one such entrepreneur during the authoring process.

Chapter 2

Strategy Overview

The first step in creating your successful federal contracting business is to clarify your personal and company goals. Generating your first revenue from the government is going to take a lot longer than what you may be accustomed to with commercial work. Knowing your "Why" and having a strategic plan in place will allow you to overcome every obstacle on your way to sustainable, profitable and predictable cash flow.

Here are a few fun facts about U.S. government contracts.

- Less than 5% of the companies in the United States do business with the U.S. government.
- The U.S. government is the largest buyer in the world. Approximately $1 billion of new contract opportunities are available to bid on each day.
- The federal government signs over 11 million contracts per year.
- About 95% of federal contracts are awarded to small-and medium-sized businesses.

Just wanting the reward of federal contracts isn't enough—you have to execute the proper strategy to achieve the goal. And, in order to do that, you must understand what motivates you.

Self-Reflection Questions

The first step to achieving business success is defining your personal and professional goals.

1. *Why do you want to go into business for yourself?*
   - Are you looking to escape your nine-to-five day job?
   - Are you tired of having a boss?
   - Are you at a place in your life where a home-based business would be beneficial?
   - Do you want to grow your small business into a more elaborate, mid- or even large-size company?

These are only some of the many reasons for going into business for yourself. The most important thing is that you know what you want and why you want it.

2. *What Are Your Company's Goals?*

Often, company goals and personal goals go hand-in-hand. I have talked to some folks whose goal it is to nurture a team of employees, who in turn have a vested interest in working together to grow the company. Those are very admirable goals to have.

Sometimes, company goals are only tied to dollar signs. Some people feel like they're going to make it when they reach a million dollars in sales, or when their net worth is a million dollars.

One of my personal goals — which is also a company goal — is to be a significant donor to my church, which participates in international feeding and medical missions. I like to be part of my church's activities, and a supporter of all the good it does.

3. *What is Your Company's Mission?*

Here is the definition of a Mission Statement, as presented on Entrepreneur.com:

"A mission statement defines what an organization is, why it exists, its reason for being. At a minimum, your mission statement should define who your primary customers are, identify the products and services you produce, and describe the geographical location in which you operate."

My company's mission is to serve the federal government by creating environments for them. We go in and survey a space with a bunch of blank walls. Then we work to understand the agency's mission, what they want to communicate and how they want to educate their clients, or other people who go into their space. From that point, we design elements, exhibits, artwork, and signage which will achieve those objectives for the agency.

We're very specific in communicating what we do. Our company's function is to design, fabricate, and install the best environments for individual government agency offices across the country. And that's what we've been built to do in a very lean fashion. Understanding your mission will allow you to build a business that supports the achievement of your specific goals.

4. *Why Does the Government Buy What You Sell?*

It's all well and good to want to work with the federal government, but to win contracts, you need to be really clear about what benefits your products or services will bring to it. The answer to that question will vary between people and businesses.

Let's use the example of Jason Maturo from It's Haul Good. The government does a lot of haul away. They're always renovating, moving into new spaces, and downsizing certain offices. They need the services Jason provides all across the country. Jason can start by hauling away for the government here in the Northern Virginia area, but he may grow himself into doing haul away services on a national level.

The government's tendency to move spaces so frequently is an asset for many small and mid-sized companies. For example, with regards to my company, every time a government building is renovated or newly occupied, is an opportunity for us to step in and customize the space. The agency wants to send certain messages which educate the people who walk into that new space about what they do.

That messaging and education are vital for government agencies because they are all vying for more funds, and thus, empowerment. Communicating what the agency is about and why they are important helps them grow.

These new offices also have practical needs. It's Haul Good, for example, can achieve a government agency's objective of removing refuse efficiently and cost-effectively. A painter with a cargo van full of brushes and equipment can go into a space and help the agency spruce it up. A flooring person can go in and give them the carpet that complements the walls and the layout and helps open up the space. An electrician can help light up the space so that everything's bright, allowing people to see well, which helps with work productivity. Even if you sell toilet paper, you can provide the best quality toilet paper at the best price and the best quality of service.

Any product or service that consumers or businesses buy in the commercial marketplace is also purchased by the federal government. From syringes to garden hoses, window cleaning to parking lot paving, paperclips to automobiles, Uncle Sam buys it and lots of it. This means that virtually any small business can become a prime federal contractor.

5. *Do You Have an Understanding of the Culture Within the Federal Government?*

There's a whole culture and mindset that surrounds the federal government and the military. My father served twenty-eight years in the U.S. Marine Corps and my wife's father served for twenty-one years in the Army. So, my wife and I have a firm understanding of the military culture, and a complete respect and admiration for everything service men and women do, which is evident in every interaction we have. It's no surprise, then, that 75% of our work deals directly with the Department of Defense. We understand the culture, we speak the language, and that helps us beat the competition for work on the federal side.

Who in your immediate social and familial network currently works for the federal government, and/or is active duty military? Those are good people for you to sit down and have coffee or lunch with, to really pick their brain to ask what their impressions of working within the federal government circle have been.

You will often hear that government workers are risk averse. This is absolutely true, and it is critical that you understand what it means from a procurement perspective. End users and contracting officers within the government want to do business with proven providers. Hiring a contractor who ultimately does not fulfill their contractual obligations makes the employee who chose them look very bad among their peers. You have to be that safe bet that's going to make that end client look good, and achieve the goals they have set out for themselves and for the unit or agency they work in.

6. *Do You Know What Federal Installations are Within Driving Distance of Your Business?*

Providing products or services to the federal government on a national level is a great goal to have. My company does so, but that wasn't my original intention. Initially, I focused on servicing clients within the Washington DC area where I am based. Your first step is to do some research to determine where every federal installation in your local area is located.

Go to the Small Business Administration website (sba.gov) and search for the Small Business Offices or Women's Business Centers in your area. I recommend visiting them in person if you need help with your research. Chances are you may know a few installations already, and those are probably good places to start.

If Los Alamos is within twenty miles of where you live, you might want to check your social media network to see if you have any unexpected connections who work there. It's a massive complex, so you might be surprised how many people in your social network are employed there. If you find that you indeed do know someone directly involved, they would be in a better position to get you a meeting with the small business liaison there, thus giving you the opportunity to present your services directly.

We'll get into more of the specific strategies later. This is more of the overview, things that you want to start thinking about, brainstorming what you want to do, and looking at your network and circle of influence to see who you could tap for additional insight.

7. *What Resources and Labor Talent Can You Devote to Government Contracting?*

Before you delve too far into the process of securing government contracts for your small business, you need to think through the resources you can give to it. What type of capital can you throw at it? Are you in a position to take on debt? Do you have some credit cards you can use?

When my wife and I first started our company, we had a lot of talent but very little cash. My wife is a self-taught graphic designer. She can design beautiful spaces that people enjoy experiencing. She's highly intelligent and mathematically inclined. Myself, I'm handy at building things and solid on the business development side. We had the small team, if you will, that we needed to launch. As for production equipment, we burned through a lot of credit to buy the printers, laminators, and all the other machines, materials and tools we needed. Not everyone will be comfortable with taking on debt, so every individual person and company must weigh the pros and the cons for themselves.

8. *What is Your Projected Timeline for Achieving a Sustainable Pipeline of Government Contracts?*

Whatever product or service you provide, if you're currently selling to consumers or to small businesses, you could go out right now and pound the pavement with flyers – or smile and dial on the telephone – to pick up new clients. These may be small jobs with unreliable payment, but they'll probably put groceries on your table that day.

On the other hand, when dealing with the federal government, it will take at least a year of preparation before you can start doing work and even longer before you receive any payment. You get paid at the tail end, after inspection's been done and receiving reports have been filed. You could be looking at an eighteen-month endeavor before you see the first payment. You really have to understand that timeline and figure out whether you can devote the time, money and energy required to power through. However, once you get to the point where you're receiving a steady stream of government contracts, you have put into place something that's going to be consistent and grow at a sustainable pace.

I caution you not to listen to some of the folks out there in Internet world, who are going to tell you, "Hey, it'll only take you a few months. There's some quick fix to it all." There's no quick fix. Like anything else you're doing in your small business, successful federal contracting requires hard work, and it takes a lot of focus and commitment.

Chapter 3

Determining Your Core Competencies

Even though the federal government buys everything under the sun, it only buys certain products or services from certain contractors. You must be very clear, in your own mind and in your communications with the government, exactly what you do well. Trying to be all things to all people is a recipe for disaster in any business.

According to Wikipedia, Core Competency is defined as the main strengths or strategic advantages of a business, including the combination of pooled knowledge and technical capacities that allow a business to be competitive in the marketplace. Here are the questions you need to answer – for yourself and for the government – in order to consistently provide high-quality products and services.

What Are Your Company's Core Competencies?

When answering this question, keep in mind that this is not the space to list all of your strengths (as I'm sure you have many.) I suggest limiting your core competency to a maximum of four key areas. However, for certain contractors, listing a single core competency may make perfect sense.

For example, if you're a painter then your sole competency is painting spaces, perhaps interior only. An architect might list three specialties such as space planning, architectural drawing, and green design. Remember, be specific to be terrific.

Why is Your Product or Service Superior to or Different from Your Competitors'?

This is a very important question as it presents the opportunity for you to shine. If your job is general contracting work and you do renovations, think about how it is that you're superior, or the best choice for the job. Is it because everybody on your team has over 15 years' experience? Is it because you have strong vendor relationships and so you get better product pricing? Is it because your systems are in place, your project management systems are in place, and you always meet deadlines? What is it that you're providing that's superior or different from your competitors?

Let's say you're a general contractor and you're equipped to work on a nationwide level. Not all GCs are, so if this is your goal, and you can work nationwide, then be sure to say so. That can be a strength that sets you apart from your competitors.

When we were first starting out, even though we were only a company of three people, we were willing to get in a car or a plane to install something in Boston, Florida, or Texas. We were different from competitors our size that weren't willing to do that. That was a strength that we used to brand ourselves as we were building our profile. We also listed our success in working on a nationwide level.

Our pricing was significantly better because many of our competitors that worked on nationwide levels had teams made up of a few hundred employees. They had a lot of payroll and overhead expenses, costs which were reflected in their proposals. We didn't have all that overhead or payroll and so our bids came in much lower.

You could be a one-person operation and get prime contracts with the federal government. Do not say to yourself, "I'm just a one-person operation. I can't do it." You can do it. There are contracts that are looking for you.

What Do Your Clients Say About You?

I recommend using Survey Monkey or another kind of surveying tool to find out what your existing clients are saying about you. Their direct reviews will help you to understand how you are perceived in the marketplace. If you want to know the truth about the level of service you provide or the quality of product that you provide, who better to ask than the people who have actually paid you to provide products and services? Survey your previous clients, and you will surely discover some new characteristics to add as you're building your branding and profile.

The Check's in the Mail

Another indicator of how your clients feel about you can be the speed of payment. Generally, if you have a lot of slow-paying clients, you are either very bad at accounts receivable or people are unhappy with the level of service you're providing. Naturally, you really want to drill down and get answers. If most are submitting payment in a quick manner all the time and happy to give you the money, well hats off to you. You definitely want to hear what they have to say so you can use that for branding. But if you get feedback that's less than positive, figure out how to make changes to improve in those areas. You're in small business to survive and thrive. It's important to grow where you can.

Which Government Agencies Buy Your Products or Services?

Do you know specifically which government agencies buy your products or services? Find out who is buying so you know where to apply. It's definitely one of those things you want to think about as this may go hand in hand with federal installations that you know of in your area. People you talk to in your sphere of influence that work at those government facilities might be able to give you some insight relative to whether your goods and services are used where they work. Don't be shy. Ask them!

The Importance of NAICS Codes

The North American Industry Classification System (NAICS) classifies business establishments for the purpose of collecting, analyzing, and publishing statistical data related to the U.S. economy. The government uses the NAICS code system to help understand what products and services different contractors provide and to identify what the agencies are looking to buy.

Go to this website, www.naics.com/search, and input the goods and services you offer to find out which NAICS codes are assigned to them. You should write down and record those numbers for now, but you will want to memorize them over time because they are that important to your company's connection to the government. You'll use them on all the proposals you write, and when you search for new requests for proposals.

Get very familiar with your NAICS codes. Print off a sheet listing them and post it by your desk so that you know them by heart when contracting officers call you. Before they award you a contract, they'll ask which NAICS codes you operate under. You'll get questions like that frequently, so don't hold up getting a contract while you shuffle around looking for the answer. Memorize those NAICS codes early on.

Chapter 4

Competitive Intelligence

One of the biggest benefits of targeting the federal government as a client is that, by law, agencies must be totally transparent about what they are buying, who they are buying from, and how much they are paying. Best of all, there are websites where all of this information is updated daily.

In this chapter I'm going to share exactly what information is available, where to find it, and how to leverage that knowledge to power the growth of your company.

What Is Your Competition Doing in the Federal Space?

The place to start is USAspending.gov, an awesome website run by the federal government. There you can learn the entities receiving each award, along with their location, the amount and transaction type, the funding agency, and any unique identifiers. When you sell to consumers or other businesses, you're always in a state of mystery, never knowing the specifics. But, when you're selling to the federal government, you know everything.

On this site, you can search for the services you provide by keyword (such as painting, carpentry, IT solutions, etc.), find out what your competitors are doing, learn what's out there in terms of trends and opportunities, and see which agencies are awarding contracts.

Be a Student of the Industry to Become a Master

If you're going to do this, do it right: Be a student of the industry. USAspending.gov is for more than doing some initial research and window shopping, saying, "Oh, heck, yeah. The government's spending millions of dollars buying what I sell—I'm all in."

Use this site on an ongoing basis. Document your top 20 competitors. Go to their websites and understand their branding. You'll find a lot of the top players within your industry have their capability statements and websites specifically structured toward federal work. From posting their NAICS codes and business designations to speaking the federal government's language, your successful competitors have strategically geared their sites to that federal client. Obviously, you don't want to duplicate them word for word, but you can utilize the essence of those messages for your website and marketing materials.

Set and Stick to Your Rituals

Set yourself a goal of an hour daily to go through USAspending.gov and dig deep into the client agencies and your competitors. Every morning, I wake up at 4:00 a.m. and write down my goals at my bathroom sink. I go into the office, read a few pages of the Bible, and look at my accounts receivable reports. For the first year, you should make a habit of spending time on this website. That daily ritual will lead to dollars in your pockets.

In a recent search I did for the keyword "exhibits" at USAspending.gov, I saw the total amount the government purchased in the last twelve months was over $3 billion, spread across 16,850 contracts as well as some grants, loans, and other things, for a total of 18,528 transactions. A rolled-up dashboard setting showed me who the recipients were, what amounts each received, from which awarding agency, along with the contract numbers. With just a click or two you can then dig down into each award to see more specific details.

What Should You Look For?

As you visit the websites of your top 20 competitors, you want to know more than just their NAICS codes and their marketing message to the government. You also want to understand how big they are, where they're located and how long they have been in business.

You also need to understand what designations they have qualified for. Are they on GSA Schedules? Do they have their SBA 8(a) designation, allowing sole sourcing capabilities? Are they a woman-owned small business? Are they in HUBZone locations? The designations you document – which your competitors are succeeding with – may be what you want to seek out for your business over time.

Even though you're in the action phase of competitive intelligence, digging in and doing the research, your goals should be evolving as well. Everything is fluid all the time. The information you gather may cause you to reassess your goals. You may want to shoot higher if you find huge federal demand for your service and a big competitive advantage in your offering. The last thing you want to do is set goals and then shove them in a corner. Invest time and effort in continuously examining your goals, and then take full, ongoing advantage of the available information.

Where Does the Information Come From?

There's another good site to become familiar with, the Federal Procurement Data System – Next Generation. A lot of the data on USAspending. gov is updated from the FPDS-NG website nightly. The FPDS-NG site provides additional information through a more sophisticated dashboard and map views that allow for a narrower, regional focus but, as a result, is a little bit cumbersome.

A daily understanding of who's buying what requires time on both these websites. If you see a lot of relevant activity from a specific agency, say, "Hey, you know what? I'm seeing the Department of State is buying an awful lot of what I sell." You might then plan to hit every one of their small business events. This information enables you to take effective action. Contrary to the shotgun approach, this competitive intelligence allows you to use your marketing dollars with more precision. The understanding you gain from these websites will help you structure your profile and branding and, ultimately, win more contracts.

There's a good book by Perry Marshall called *80/20 Sales and Marketing: The Definitive Guide to Working Less and Making More.* Marshall goes into the rule of 80/20—20% of your clients will yield 80% of your profit. Keep that in mind when building your profile and understanding who to target. These sites are going to tell you who's buying the most of what you sell. There should be little question which agencies to approach if you're spending the necessary time on USAspending.gov and FPDS.gov.

Are There Other, More Precise Ways to Search?

Continuing with our previous example, I can search for the keyword, "exhibits," on the FPDS-NG website to find the top 10 agencies buying what I offer. How great is that? They are fully providing, in a very structured manner, the top 10 clients I should target.

But a more specific, refined search will result by using NAICS codes. Go to the NAICS code website, find the code or codes that most closely match your product or service. Then use FPDS-NG to look up the agencies that are buying the most of those NAICS codes. This will result in a more refined top 10 list, than results from a general search with potentially overlapping categories. You will also see all your competitors there, including the top 10 vendors' full names.

What Does All This Cost?

All the marketing companies in this world want to sell you things. As a small business, everybody wants your money, all the time. But what I have described in this chapter is an endless stream of powerful competitive data for which you won't pay a penny.

There are a lot of consultants, training companies and gurus who will tell you, "Hey, follow these steps to sell to the federal government." But I am that small guy who struggled to learn all this and operated out of his basement, accumulated hundreds of thousands of dollars in debt, barely making payroll on schedule, countless times. Having started small and then learned how to obtain multi-million dollar contracts—four- or five-year blanket purchase agreements—I put this together to be of service, so you could grow your small business and experience longevity, sustainability, and increased profit for yourself and your employees.

Is There Value in Relational Business and Working with Competitors?

Let's return to my search on the word "exhibits" on the USAspending.gov website. Among recent awards I see that KLB received a $5,200 contract, Universal got a $365,000 award, and VIP got a $4,500 project. A little more digging reveals that Universal just got their contract last week. Hmm.

I might want to contact them to say, "Hey, can I sub for you? I see you're in California, but this job's in Washington, DC, which is 20 miles from where we're based. Can I assist with installation? That will cut down on your travel time and expense." In the federal space, competitors become friends and teaming partners all the time. On many of the larger contracts, there's enough pie to go around.

What would be even more amazing is to approach that larger competitor or teaming partner and say, "Hey look, I'm making a concerted effort to sell to the federal government on a prime level. I'm going to need your resources to back me up." And then you'll be able to reciprocate and deliver jobs back to them. How incredible would that be for your relationship with that company?

I know the idea of research can turn a lot of people off because you're in the "do" mode. You're busy, you have clients calling, and you've got new proposals to pump out. You're busy with the banker, the attorney, the CPA, etc. But this is not so much research as it is molding your future. Don't take this lightly. Make it part of your daily ritual. Learn what's out there.

Chapter 5

Your MAP (Massive Action Plan)

When Ruth and I first started out in business, we put together a comprehensive marketing plan. But I wasn't satisfied with it. What I needed was an action plan, a massive action plan that would skyrocket our sales and income. In order to be effective, it had to be fluid and ever-moving, evolving as we traveled through our entrepreneurial journey.

Ruth, who's much smarter than me, said, "Oh, it will be our MAP. Our Massive Action Plan." I had never picked up on that, but she was absolutely right, as usual.

Your MAP begins with your marketing plan, but goes much further, into how you're going to implement that plan with the correct elements of rapid success.

Your Massive Action Plan (MAP)

Marketing Plan:

The worst thing you can do as a business owner is to not be known. If you're not known, nobody can find you to give you money. Nobody can find you to partner with you. You're in your own little cave.

When Ruth and I started our company, we were extremely small. The larger exhibit and signage companies would ignore us and even belittle us. They couldn't understand why we, a small new firm with limited expertise and resources, would be bidding on the same prime federal contracts they were bidding on. They were used to the small circle of people they knew and understood and regularly competed against. Here I was, a newbie who wasn't looking to work with them. I just wanted their clients.

Over the years, I chipped away at their client base. Now they know me and I'm inside the circle. Now I'm getting calls to partner. Now things are different. I don't hold grudges. Let's let bygones be bygones and make some money.

All of this happened because I had a marketing plan.

Your Profile and Reputation

It's critical that you understand what your strengths are. What is your core competency? What are you good at? What do you do that's superior to what your competitors do, or different from what they do? Are you nationwide? What is the geographical range that you can operate within? Who are you selling to? All of these factors are going to impact how you build your profile and reputation.

Associations and Social Media

Begin looking at associations and social media groups to join to help you assemble your tribe, build your network. You need to know your competitors. You need to know your peers – other government contractors that you need to begin talking shop with. You're really creating a whole new lifestyle for yourself. Government contracting is very much a lifestyle with social circles you need to become part of.

Connect with government people on social platforms like Facebook and LinkedIn. Then, when they see your proposal come across their desk, they'll recognize your name because you've branded yourself well.

Small Business Events

Federal agencies host events for small businesses where you can build relationships with contract officers, managers and end users within the agencies you want to target. You need to put these events on your calendar every month and attend them religiously.

Pipeline Building

As you hone your profile and build your communities by participating in government contracting associations and attending small business events, you will start to grow a pipeline of relationships and activity. For example, when you go to an agency-sponsored event, they may tell you when they will have a requirement coming out. That goes in your pipeline. When you participate in association events or online communities, you will meet potential partners. Someone will say "Hey, we could team on this because I'm a general contractor, and I need a painter, and you happen to be a painter." That person and that opportunity go into your pipeline.

You must make a commitment to all five elements of your MAP. What are you willing to commit in terms of labor and resources to social media, participation with associations, research and attendance at small business events, and management of your pipeline? Each piece needs an individual game plan and attention on an ongoing basis. It's going to take ongoing effort — you're going to have to devote resources to ensure that you keep this whole cycle of life in motion at all times. But this will yield dollars in your pocket.

To effectively implement your MAP, you need to look at the following:

Revenue Goals

If you're currently doing $200,000 in annual gross revenue with commercial clients and/or consumers, what's your revenue goal going to be for government work? Is your goal to do $800,000 with federal clients after 18 months while maintaining the $200,000 with commercial and consumer clients? That might be more under the heading of business mix objectives, but it should roll up to your overall revenue goals as well.

Budget Forecasting

You need to understand what your fixed expenses are. Your variable expenses will increase as you do more outreach with the federal government. It's just inevitable. You might need to take on a committed salesperson that's going to help you grow the federal space. Again, that would be something you need to budget for.

Small Business Designations

We'll cover this topic in more detail in another chapter, but I wanted to touch on it briefly here as well. If you qualify as a small business, a woman-owned business, a veteran-owned business, etc. you will be eligible to receive priority consideration as a bidder on federal contracts. There are even certain contracts which are set aside solely for specific designations. Visit the Small Business Administration website at https://www.sba.gov/ and learn what small business designations you might qualify for.

You need a good solid year of federal contracting work under your belt before you reach out and start trying to obtain any designations. A majority of the designating bodies will want to know what your past performance is with the federal government because the government culture is very risk averse. The designations are in place to help small businesses obtain federal contracts or access federal contracts. But a designation does not guarantee that you will win a contract or perform successfully. The federal buyers need to know that you have the resources and expertise to perform on those projects and not go under midway.

Geographic Reach

Are you only going to provide your goods and services in your local area, regionally or nationwide? Let's say my company has four core competencies. Initially, when we were very small, I'd say I could deliver all four services locally within the Washington DC area; but was only willing to offer three of those four services nationwide. I was not willing to do signage on a nationwide level because I didn't have the staffing, equipment or resources. I wouldn't have been competitive on a nationwide level. Understand what your business mix objectives are between commercial and federal government clients, and what your geographic reach will be given the core competencies that you possess.

Teaming Objectives

As you build and grow your network through associations, social media and small business events, you'll meet a lot of potential teaming partners, competitors and peers that you may wish to subcontract work to – or from. You'll be in rooms full of people that want to do business with the federal government. So you need to be clear on your teaming objectives: do you want to find one or more teaming partners right out of the gate or do you want to pick them up as requirements come out which require expertise or resources you don't have? You may have expertise with painting, but there may be both painting and handyman requirements in a given contract. You'll need to seek out someone with handyman capabilities to satisfy that requirement.

Outsourcing and Tools

You also need to intelligently outsource tasks and use technology to support your MAP. Use QuickBooks online for your accounting. Use a project management tool like Trello or Basecamp. There are a number of cloud-based tools that allow other team members to log in remotely. Think of what type of technology is going to support your performance.

The good news in today's world is there are many cloud-based resources that are dirt cheap to employ. They replace the need for extra labor and minimize wasted time. You just need to understand what resources are out there. I've frequently use Fiverr.com, where you can get labor to help you with essentially any task, performed by skilled and dedicated people around the world.

I have a virtual assistant in another country that does all my bookkeeping. I used to pay ten times the amount to have a bookkeeper do it locally. It would take them three weeks to do the work that it takes my virtual assistant about three days to do. It's a much more professional delivery, and it's a tenth of the cost. They're making me more efficient and saving me more money. Set that up now.

Organization Structures

As you brainstorm and put you MAP together, you're going to question many of the structures you have in place now. And you should. You should look to be lean and mean, make the adjustments, and not just make the adjustments but commit to them. That's the key. That's where many of people fall short and then give up on government work. They get into month eight, and haven't gotten a federal penny. They get frustrated and they just drop out. They decide commercial work is quick money; it's down and dirty. They get paid right away, so they decide to go back to what they know. Yet, they were much closer than they knew to getting the end game of federal work, just before they gave up.

Now is the time to move outside your comfort zone. Figure out a way to go massive with it. I mean 10X your goal, as Grant Cardone would tell you. Go for a million. Forget $200k, go for $2 million. Forget $2 million, go for $20 million. You can see on USASpending.gov that there are millions of dollars in contracts being let every day. About 95% of the companies getting them are small to midsize. It's all lined up for you. It's just on you to do that massive action plan and carve yourself in. Nobody's going to do that for you.

As you go down your journey to selling to the federal government, you will meet consultants who have never received a federal contract in their name try to sell you on a panacea. They say they can tell you how to get up and running because they have a database of federal buyers. Other folks out there teaching federal contracting have worked for a large company like Lockheed Martin or BAE but have never taken the risks you have as an entrepreneur. Consider yourself warned.

By the way, those big companies don't like people like me and you because we're cutting them out by selling to the federal buyer on a prime level. We don't need them. We don't need their bloated overhead. We don't need the crumbs they'll give us. We go straight to the government client. The big companies want to dominate the industry. Or they want to use the small guy for the crumbs, and then pay late after 90 days. I don't partner with them. I don't sub for them and neither should you. With your MAP, you can bypass that route and become your own prime federal contractor.

Your Guerrilla Marketing Plan

Now that you know the components of the MAP, let's dig into the actual marketing plan piece. I use Guerrilla Marking, the approach to marketing created by Steven Levinson and made famous in his book of the same name. Levinson's message is that your marketing plan should be one page, very short and clear. There are just a few points you should hit. It shouldn't be a document that is so heavy you kick it off to the side. It should be something you can post right by your desk where you spend most of your day.

Here is how to write your one-page Guerilla Marketing Plan:

1. The first sentence tells the purpose of the marketing strategy
2. The second sentence tells how you'll achieve this purpose
3. The third describes your target market — or markets
4. The forth lists the marketing weapons you'll use
5. The fifth describes your niche and position
6. The sixth is your identity
7. The seventh is your budget, expressed as a percentage of your projected gross revenue

Before You Write Your Guerilla Marketing Plan

Federal target marketing is easy. Just spend some time on USASpending.gov learning which agencies buy the most of what you sell. Next, determine what marketing weapons you will employ to connect with the buyers at those agencies and let them know about how your company can serve them.

Do you have a sales person? Can they devote the full-time attention that's needed to get up and running with government sales as soon as possible? No? Okay, well how can you outsource that? How can you bring someone on, on a commission-only basis? Can you take on a partner that can allow you to develop this new business model?

Next you need to consider how to position yourself in the minds of federal buyers, alongside – or apart from – your competition. What's your niche? What's your position? What's your identity? You need to do this self-reflection upfront because you need to know these answers. You should know your niche by your NAICS code(s). You should know your identity based upon your core competencies.

You should know your marketing budget. You need to put thought into the resources you can commit. Sometimes you can express that as a percentage of your projected gross revenue. If you want to generate $2 million in top-line revenue, then maybe your marketing budget needs to be $200k, 10% of your gross revenue.

These are questions you must ask yourself if you want to achieve a massive transformation. Now let's start writing your Guerilla Marketing Plan.

Sentence One: Purpose Statement

Your purpose statement can be a specific income goal or something more subjective. My goal is to be the largest donor at my church because of the international missions they perform. That's my why. That's why I would 10X my income goal. That's why I would transform my business operations and sell to the federal government instead of commercial clients.

I have four children at home. My wife stays at home with them and is starting to home school. Providing my family a lifestyle that's comfortable is another one of my whys. I can't meet all of my whys on $200k a year. On $2 million, perhaps. I need to hit certain gross revenue levels and profit margin levels in order to satisfy all my whys.

If you don't have strong conviction with your whys, you're not going to make it happen. You'll be the month eight person that just says, "You know what? I can't do this anymore." The last thing I want for anybody reading this book is to try federal contracting for a few months and then quit. I'm giving you everything here you need to succeed. But only you can find the perseverance required to reach the pot of gold at the end of the rainbow.

You cannot overlook the importance of participation in local government contract associations, or using social media, because learning is earning. You need to be a student of the industry and fully commit to maximize revenue. If you're going to 10X your goals, but you're not going to 10X your action to achieve your goals, what's the point? There is no point. If you're going to 10X your goals, if you're going to 10X your vision, then really go for it. Make all your actions speak to that.

I primarily serve the Department of Defense because they are the largest buyer of what I provide. I understand the military culture and I have a strong record of past performance with DoD. The purpose of my marketing strategy is to grow deeper within military bases and other DoD components.

Sentence Two: How Will You Achieve Your Objective?

We're going to go back to that MAP cycle of life. You're going to achieve your marketing objective through commitment to research on USASpending. gov, commitment to branding, and social media, commitment to joining and participating in contracting associations, attending small business events and regularly performing outreach, making phone calls to government clients and introducing yourself.

Implementing your federal marketing plan cannot be done by your current salesperson, who is already working eight hours per day serving commercial clients. You can't say, "Hey, carve out an hour a day to get up and running with federal sales, and I'll check back in a year to see how it's going."

That's just not going to work. You need full-time commitment for this to work the way you need it to work.

For example, I'm going to devote Betsy, who works in sales, to federal. I'm going to cut her out of commercial sales and I'm going to give her a five-hour window. Every day, she's going to spend one hour on USASpending.gov collecting competitive intelligence. She's going to spend two hours cold calling government clients. She's going to spend one hour on social media, and she's going to spend one hour building her pipeline and working proposals. That is the marketing strategy. That is the resource. That's what I'm going to throw at it to ensure this will be a success. That's what I visualize for the marketing strategy.

Networking and the Government Marketing Lifestyle

Living the government lifestyle is part of your marketing strategy. The lifestyle you have now is that of a small business owner. You have friends from before you became a small business owner, and you've been gradually acquiring more friends that own small businesses. You're probably spending more time now with the small business owners than with the friends you met at your corporate job. When you get together with other business owners, you talk shop about the industry, things that are affecting you, some marketing plans. There are probably some general small business events you attend, like the Chamber of Commerce or Business

Networking International (BNI). That's your small business owner lifestyle circle of influence.

With government contracting, you're going to replace all of that with fellow government contractors or teaming partners. It's just a whole new circle of influence that you'll be creating around yourself.

I still have my small business friends. But time is limited, and you have to use it wisely. I choose to use it to maintain a circle of influence with peers and partners that can help grow my government contracting business. As they help me grow, I can grow my family and everyone around me. That's what's important to me.

Just like 10Xing your revenue, you need to 10X your culture. Think of the network you've built for yourself up to this point, the people, the peers, et cetera. The people you see at the Chamber of Commerce, what are they doing gross revenue-wise? I would venture to say that, at the Chamber of Commerce, most members' top line revenue is maybe $200k to $300k. You need to re-identify yourself as a government contractor and start connecting with people who do $100 million in business. I connect with them quite often.

I'm not saying don't be friends with someone because they're doing $200k. But if you want to get to that point where you're doing $10 million, $20 million, or $100 million, then you need to start associating yourself and spending time and resources connecting with those people that are doing what you want to do.

Build your identity, 10X your identity, re-label yourself. Your mindset should be "We are a government contracting firm. We have aspirations of $20 million a year. The reason we're going to hit that is because we have created and implemented a massive action plan, and we are fully committed to making it work."

Someone who makes $100 million has very strong rituals in place. They wake up early before everyone else. They're sending emails off to set agendas for everyone around them. They're not waiting for the end of fiscal year to throw out some bids. They're working January 1st on what's going to transpire September 30th. They're well ahead. They're leading from in front. They're creating the whole process and monitoring it to ensure that it occurs the way they visualized it because they're on top of it on a daily basis.

The takeaway from the government lifestyle is that there are people in your industry that are doing one hundred times what you're doing in revenue. You need to find those people, and you can use USASpending.gov to do that. You need to connect with those people. You need to see which associations they're members of, which small business events they're going to, where they are on LinkedIn and Facebook. You need to be where they are today, if you want to be where they are in the future.

Chapter 6

Profile and Reputation

You have your massive action plan in place. Your next step is to customize your LinkedIn profile to begin building your online identity, as well as your offline reputation, as a federal contractor. Most of the people you will want to connect with (federal buyers and fellow contractors) are going to be in the US, but there are many international entities and organizations that sell to the US federal government too. You will be jumping onto a national/international scene when you join LinkedIn contractor groups.

Business Development & Capture Management, Federal Government Contracting ♦ Secret Clearance ♦ 10+ years of experience

The Catholic University of America, Columbus School of Law

Washington D.C. Metro Area · 500+ 👥

Connect | View in Sales Navigator | More...

The graphic above is a snapshot I took of a government contractor's personal LinkedIn profile, and I think it provides a good description to model yours after. This person lists his or herself as focusing on business development and capture management, two terms that are widely used in the government space. Business development is another word for a sales person. Capture managers are the people who bring in new projects.

The specific focus of their profile is federal government contracting. The person holds a secret security clearance and has 10 plus years of experience. These items basically say, "My character is impeccable, I have a long-term experience in government contracting, and this is my sole focus." And then you can scroll down and read their detailed description.

CAPTURE MANAGEMENT • BUSINESS DEVELOPMENT • PROPOSAL WRITING
I have a passion for developing themes, strategies, and value propositions that harness a company's past performance and technical capabilities to win new business in the federal government contracting space.

My experience spans the entire business development lifecycle, supporting opportunity identification, marketing, capture management, and proposal writing. Results:

• Contributed to team wins of $3.7+ billion in awards in 5 years, and developed and supported business cases to support strategic initiatives into adjacent markets.

Here's another example of a great LinkedIn profile for a federal contractor. This is the company profile for an SBA certified small disadvantaged business. This profile demonstrates the importance of designations and why you should feature them prominently in your LinkedIn profile.

Native American SBA 8a Certified Small Disadvantaged Business, Federal Government Contracting

Native American SBA 8a • George Mason University
Washington D.C. Metro Area • 500+ 🏢

Connect   View in Sales Navigator   More...

They also have an excellent description of what their looking for included in their LinkedIn profile.

████████████████ is a Native American owned SBA 8a certified small disadvantaged business.

I am actively seeking reliable and aggressive teaming partners and potential joint venture partners for whom our relationship is mutually beneficial. You will find us capable, mobile, and also aggressive not only in the pursuit of a contract, but also in its fulfillment. We are based in the Washington, D.C. area and have access to the headquarters and SDBU's of all federal agencies. I would welcome the chance to talk with you further about future opportunities to

Being truthful in your profile is very important — you are building a reputation on LinkedIn in which you want to be seen as honest and full of integrity. If you are currently in the midst of changing your focus to federal government, and/or you've only been in business for a short period of time, you can still say "Business development focused on the federal government." Just be truthful about your level of experience.

I have a passion for developing themed strategies and value propositions that harness my company's past performance and technical capabilities to win new business in the federal government space. You can be as descriptive as possible, but you want to also be strategic and stay on theme. You may even want to have a few of your fellow government contracting peers look over your description and give you some insight.

As soon as you're set up on LinkedIn, one of the first things you want to do is go under the group setting (My Groups) and join some federal contracting communities. Just type "federal contracting" in the search window and select "Groups." Hit enter and watch what happens. There are many such groups on LinkedIn and many members in each group. The Government Contracting Community group alone has almost 12,000 members.

I don't know any other setting where you could more easily connect with thousands of your fellow contractors so easily. You need to spend time every day on LinkedIn, contributing in the groups, reading through posts, responding to people's posts, and really getting a sense for the community. Providing valuable contributions will aid in developing your reputation, so make sure you are adding value every day.

Your new LinkedIn profile is going to go a long way toward reinventing or redefining your identity and helping you build a solid reputation as a federal contractor online. I'm not dogging anyone in a Chamber of Commerce, there are a lot of great, viable businesses there and a lot of good people I've known through the Chamber. But now you're going to spend more effort and energy on connecting with people who, like you, are focused on government contracting.

To assess the impact of your investment of time on LinkedIn, you should be measuring everything. Track the groups you join, the people you're connecting with, and the people you view as thought leaders (people that are putting out good articles and good comments, who you feel you can really learn from). Which of those connections and relationships are getting you closer to bid opportunities? Making friends with someone on LinkedIn that you view as a thought leader, an expert in government contracting, could go a long way to help you.

During your first five years in federal contracting, you need to get your name out there as much as possible. When I initially started government contracting, I was active in about ten LinkedIn groups, several associations and some local in-person organizations. I would participate in the groups and sponsor events to get my name out there as well.

You'll find as your reputation grows — as you do what you say you're going to do and as you participate in the groups — there will be a snowball effect that will allow you to back away a little bit over time. I'm not nearly as active as I used to be. But initially you need to be all in and getting exposure. In order for federal buyers to choose your company, they need to know who you are in the federal space.

Consistent Graphic Branding

When I was setting everything up, I found two business sites that were very affordable solutions for help with my marketing plan. The first one is Fiverr.com. I use Fiverr regularly to find everything from designers to help with media and website design to bookkeeping. You name it, you can find it there. You'll find people located all over the world (many in Pakistan and in India). They will work for you at a much more affordable price. I have also found the level of service to be incredible. I've had a few bad experiences, but everything got corrected, and for the most part I recommend going to this site.

4over.com is a printing service out of California, much like Vistaprint.com. I find them to be extremely affordable, and the quality is good. At the time this book was written, I paid $80 for 1,000 double-sided full color business cards with laminate on one side. They're fast and easy to work with, and they sell a number of different marketing services.

If you're waiting a few weeks at your local printer or graphic designer, that's too long. Speed is the new competitive advantage. With time being short on this earth, make speed your friend. As I always say, time is either your enemy or your friend, depending on how you use it.

In the next chapter I will go into more detail about what type of marketing materials you need. I cannot overstate the importance of having professional design and printing done for business cards and one-page capability statements, which you'll need whenever you meet a peer or competitor in the industry. You will also bring your printed capability statement with you to small business events and will include it with your bid whenever you're handing in a physical response to an RFP (request for proposal).

If you have been following my advice up to this point, you have dramatically improved your odds of federal contracting success without spending a dime – except for the cost of this book! You've completely transformed the way you look at and think about your company. You're beginning to transform your online identity and profile, as well as your offline identity and reputation. You've done all the competitive intelligence, you know who your best buyers are in the federal space, who your biggest competitors and potential teaming partners are. And you still have not spent one penny.

It's very important to know that a lot of what I'm covering in this book is not going to involve spending money. Everything is out there for you. All that's required is for you to commit to success, work hard and put all the pieces together.

Chapter 7

Associations and Social Media

This chapter is all about establishing your brand and building your network through associations and social media.

You're a government contractor now: start building your network and having fun! There are a lot of other people out there who are passionate about government contracting. Getting together creates an enjoyable atmosphere where you can share success stories, systems and tips that have worked for you, while gaining valuable insight into what others have learned. Use these lessons to hone what you do and learn how to better yourself and your company.

There are several government contracting associations you should be aware of. AFCEA (The Armed Forces Communications and Electronics Association) is a huge association with many regional offices that provide resources, live training and networking opportunities. You can find out more at afcea.org.

GovCon.net, and GovernmentContractors.org are associations you should also look into. They present a lot of webinars which are great ways to maintain your education in the federal contracting industry. Engaging with these associations also helps you build your network of peers, acquaintances, friends and associates.

It isn't enough for you to put your plan together, do all the competitive intelligence, and then go after bids on your own. You also need the social media aspect because it validates you, it educates you, and it prepares you with all the information and tips you need to write that winning proposal.

Being active in associations gives you insights that will help you better position yourself to win awards. It's one thing to go out and find RFP's to bid on – that part is easy. It's an entirely different task to put out a good, solid proposal that's going to appeal to a risk-averse government procurement officer. Getting involved with these associations will hone your skills and prepare you to win these bids.

Associations take time, money, and focus. This is the first part of the entire process I am presenting in this book that requires you to spend some money. Don't skip it. And don't just be a run-of-the-mill member. Become a sponsor for individual events or an annual sponsor who is listed on the association's website. That level of involvement on your part shows your commitment and legitimacy in the contracting world.

Remember that you want to increase your speed towards that end goal of winning contracts. That's why you're reading this book, so you don't have to reinvent the wheel and figure it all out on your own. Make speed your friend in this area as well. Use these associations to help you get contracts in the door quickly.

Your involvement in associations and social media is an area where you need to remember how valuable your time is, and what activities are worth your time investment. As a small business owner, you're doing the banking, the systems, the labor, and all of the various processes that make up a business. You should budget and plan for your involvement in associations and social media along with those everyday tasks.

I'm not the type of person who will tell you, "I don't have the time." That isn't the issue. The question is whether I see the value of investing a portion of my valuable time into whatever someone may be proposing. That's where self-reflection comes into play. You need to really analyze all the areas where you're spending time, from the small business groups you're participating in, all the way to whether you watch TV shows at night.

You need to start building your lifestyle around this whole process. Make time to engage in social media for business and make these connections. Budget the time required to make phone calls to government folks and procurement officers. Go to small business events and follow up on the connections you make there. Create that in-person face time with local government contracting associations to really tie everything together. You will hear about things at these events that you would never know about if you didn't have that personal interaction.

I cannot over-emphasize the value of your time. It's a finite resource that needs to be treasured and stewarded with respect. There are always things that I could cut out of my day and replace with an activity that would be more lucrative for me, my business, and my family. This is why I don't watch TV. There are other activities which are more valuable uses of my time.

GovCon on Facebook

You probably wouldn't believe it but Government contracting, or GovCon for short, is everywhere on Facebook. Just type in a key phrase like "government contracting," "government contractors' association," or simply "GovCon" into the search box and you'll be surprised at how much you find. There are literally more groups there than you could ever hope to become involved with. But I have to say that I am partial to the "Secrets to Winning Government Contracts" group on Facebook.

Remember that when you use social media for business, your social media profile is an extension of yourself. I don't use my Facebook for connecting with friends and family as much as I do to establish my identity in the federal space and build relationships with buyers, peers and potential teaming partners.

It's unreal how much business gets done over Facebook. When you go to events with government contractors, you should follow up by connecting with them on social media. The purpose of attending these events isn't to just go out once a month and see what Fred is up to. You want to connect with Fred on Facebook so that you'll later see that his status says "Hey, just landed a four-year BPA (blanket purchase agreement) at this agency! I'm so excited! I'm going to celebrate tonight with my wife, June." This is where you not only meet people, but you connect with them on a much deeper level. That opens avenues for work for yourself. That's how you should view Facebook, LinkedIn, and other social platforms.

Finding Local Associations

Do a Google search for government contracting associations in the city where you live. If one doesn't already exist, consider starting one. That's an opportunity to be a thought leader and gain credibility, just by taking the initiative to start an organization. You never know who you might meet by doing that.

I've done flooring, drywall, and painting work from the connections I've made this way. There's a whole host of other projects outside of my core competencies that I've been able to grow into just based on knowing other government contractors and having relationships in place. They saw a requirement, needed expertise, and knew I could help. A lot of this stuff isn't advertised. It's all through connections on social media and associations I'm a part of.

As I mentioned earlier, when you type in "government contracting" on Facebook, you'll find more groups than you know what to do with. Realize that you're not going to be able to be active in all of these groups. Join as many of them as interest you, then slowly work through the groups and narrow them down to the ones where there is a personality connection between you and the other members. After you sift through the 20 groups you joined, you may find that only two of them really pertain to your industry and have people that are active and engaged in topics that are of interest to you. This is where you focus your time.

When you put yourself out there as a freshly minted federal contractor on Facebook, you may feel like you're a teenage girl or boy again. "Hi, I'm Jason. I'm a new guy just getting into the federal contracting world. Any tips for a newbie?" Track and record the groups that provide an impact or that you think could be significant to you, as well as the people you think could be beneficial to the growth of your business. Record all this in a customer relations management (CRM) system like Salesforce.com, so you can follow up and stay in touch. Connect with people on social media and then talk to them. Just give them a call, introduce yourself, and then have a chat about the industry and how you could potentially work together. You never know where it will lead. Sometimes it goes nowhere, but many times the results are amazing. Following this process consistently has definitely led to dollars in my pocket.

Building a network through associations and social media is an area where you have to frontload your effort. My wife and I are on our fourth child, and the age range is 5, 3, 2 and newborn. I'm not nearly as active in associations or on social media as I used to be. But I did the social media thing for countless hours throughout the early years. This is how we've built our business, and we have a lot of contracts and contacts that we gained from social media that we still utilize on a regular basis. Since we spent so much time developing those connections early on, our company is more mature and profitable at the ten-year-plus point and we don't have to commit as much time to social media now. Our workload has shifted to home and a different focus within our company.

Remember that this book is written for the person who is establishing him or herself and doing what it takes to win their first government contracts. At this point in your business, you need to allot some serious time to your involvement with associations and social media. That isn't to say you can't drink a beer while you're on social media or go through Facebook while NCIS is playing in the background. You can be flexible, but ultimately you need to invest the time to get this done.

Martin and Ruth meet with Senator John Kerry on Capitol Hill in the late 2000s

Martin receives Seven Seals Award from the
Employer Support of the Guard and Reserve in 2016

Helping raise money for the Community Business
Partnership in 2006

Martin giving a tour of the Pentagon to
his student Chaim Ekstein in 2017

Training Investors and Small Business Owners in 2018

Chapter 8

Small Business Events

This chapter's focus is small business events, or industry days, which are produced by government agencies to connect with small contractors like you and me. Up to this point we have covered all of your first steps: having a plan, building your branding, getting on social media, and joining some government contracting associations. Now you're ready to hit the streets, to go out and meet federal buyers face to face.

The first step is to go to FedBizOpps.gov, a very popular website where most government contracting opportunities are listed, along with many small business events. Agencies host these events as an outreach effort to find small businesses that are capable of performing requirements that the agencies either currently have or know they will have in the future. These events are awesome opportunities to meet buyers and end users, and learn how you can help them.

When you go to FedBizOpps.gov you will see a keyword section. Type in "small business event," "industry days, "or "OSDBU," which is the Office of Small, Disadvantaged Business and Utilization, the small business arm for each of the agencies. After your search results appear on the screen, sift through and find the agencies that are the most frequent buyers of the products and services you provide. For example, if the Department of State is doing the bulk of the buying for what you provide, you want to focus on industry days sponsored by the Department of State.

If you're not sure which ones you should attend, then go to as many as your budget will allow. I've flown around the country when I knew that the industry days were being held by clients of mine and requirements were coming out in my area of expertise. The listings for these events will include small business officers, the procurement officers that actually put out the notices.

Click on the event link and you'll see the small business officers listed. Reach out to them and find out if they're going to be discussing or advertising the kind of requirements you're looking for. They normally have an understanding of who they're seeking and what kind of service or product requirements they need to fill. Doing this allows you to find out if there's anything that is applicable to you before spending the money to attend the event.

You need to keep in mind who the big buyers in your industry are. You may call the small business person who is running the event and get a response that says they're not looking for what you provide. If you know that, in spite of what you were just told, this department tends to buy a lot of what you provide, you still want to attend the industry day to meet all of the program managers and contracting officers. Get their contact information and enter it into your CRM. Keep in touch by calling them over the next few months. You never know when a requirement will pop up.

One of the keys here is preparation, which starts with getting your Dun and Bradstreet number and registering on Sam.gov. Do that upfront, because you're going to need have both of those elements in place in order to do business with the federal government. Next, create a business card that shows your branding as a player in the federal contracting space. Develop a capabilities statement with all your NAICS codes and examples of past performance, including pictures of work you've done. You also want to apply to receive as many small business designations as possible.

You could walk in having not done any of the preparation I'm telling you to do, but the response you're going to get when you talk to the procurement officers is to do all the things you've just read here. However, if you walk in and say: "Here's my business card. I serve the federal government with signage and exhibits. Here is my capabilities statement, and I'm already registered on Sam.gov and FedBizOpps. I'm certified by the SBA as an 8(a) company." This shows them you're ready to do business and the conversation then centers around opportunities that are available now, or who you can talk to in the future to discuss opportunities and services you can provide. It's a much more pointed conversation.

This is a full-time focus, a full-time job, and a full-time commitment. You need to question yourself: do you have the resources to hire a full-time salesperson, or how can you get the resources to make this a priority for you and your business?

One of your goals at a small business event or industry day is to meet with the small business representative. They're usually out of the OSDBU office. The OSDBU's job is to understand the agency forecast, where the money is going to be spent, what types of contracts are going to come out, and which small business designations they're going to use. Your job is to know the OSDBU. The OSDBU representatives should be heavily tracked in your CRM system, and you should be calling on them on a regular basis.

You also want to meet with contracting officers, program managers, and influencers at these events. Contracting officers are the people facilitating the contract—they're not the end user. They're looking for contractors with goals that align with their projects, or specific types of businesses, such as women-owned businesses, or HUBZone, 8a businesses, those that work through a GSA schedule or GPO, et cetera. They're the ones putting all the pieces together and ensuring funding is in place to issue the award for the contract. Federal contracting officers are entirely different than program managers or end users. Thinking of getting your GSA Schedule or filing for a small business designation, email me at info@govcon.win and I'll send you a good contact I personally used to get setup with my GSA schedule.

The program or project managers are the ones who will be overseeing the contract once it is awarded. The influencers are the end users, the ones who need the work to be done. Sometimes the program managers and influencers are the same and sometimes they're different individuals.

When you meet these people, you want to get down to business. You aren't there to get them to tell you the obvious or rehash all of the steps I've told you to take. You want to talk business that is going to be feeding your family and your employees' families. You should attend as many of these events as possible because you'll see the same government contracting peers at a lot of these events. This is a good time to find teaming partners.

I've also found a lot of government contractors I could do business with by attending these events. Many of these contractors have the same needs the government does and you may be able to sell to them as well. This is a potential source of lower-hanging fruit. Remember that I gave you that one-year commitment you're going to need to make, and you need 18 months before you're really going to see the effects of your efforts. Some of these government contractors may have immediate needs for what you do that could help ease the financial burden you're taking on of selling to the federal government and the timeline that requires. Bottom line is to follow all the steps I've outlined in this book and you should begin to receive federal contracts in within 12 months. It took me 2 years to start receiving federal contracts, but I was starting without any guidance while spending a lot of time just figuring things out that I've laid out in this book.

Regarding fellow government contractors, you want all of these people to know your name and capabilities so that when a requirement comes out, they call you. That's why you put the plan in place: you're doing all of the branding and profile work, so people can know you. You're on social media and part of associations so they can know you. You're at small business events so they can know you. All this effort is so you can be seen and remembered when the requirements come out that match your capabilities.

Chapter 9

Building Your Pipeline

In this chapter we're going to be talking about Building Your Pipeline, the last stage of your Massive Action Plan Life Cycle. Even though your MAP is cyclical, it really acts like a funnel because, if you're doing everything I've taught you, placing all the ingredients correctly at the top, the output should be a very healthy pipeline projects and revenue that will sustain your business and give you a report card of how you're doing.

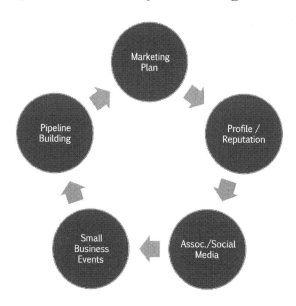

Building your pipeline is a matter of taking the connections you've made through social media, associations and small business events, and placing them in your CRM to track your past communications and schedule future outreach. Your pipeline is made up of people, phone calls, RFPs and proposals that are moving toward the finish line of awarded contracts.

You want to gather as much contact information as possible from the people you're meeting, including their name, the name of the agency or company they work for, their title, physical/mailing address, email address, phone numbers, social media platforms that they are on, etc. Your CRM should have this information on contracting officers, program managers, OSBDU folks and other contractors like yourself.

You're likely to find all of these people at small business events, including end users searching for vendors to recommend to program managers, and program managers. researching the pool of resources available to fill current or future requirements of their agency or division. They're not hosting these industry days for show. They have real dollars that they need to spend. They want to know who's ready to receive those dollars and who has the expertise to perform for those dollars.

Tracking Your Pipeline

Track and monitor your sales outreach activity on a daily basis. I do this for myself to this day. As

I've mentioned, I may be more hands-off these days with social media because I have the four little ones aged 5 and under. Also, our business is mature now and we have a lot of long-term contracts in place. But, as far as managing my pipeline is concerned, I continue to monitor it on a daily basis. I see where the sales folks need to start calling during the day. I track how many calls they've made, how many proposals they've sent out daily and how many proposals they're working on.

You can get as fancy and high-tech as you'd like when creating your pipeline tracking system, but it really doesn't need to be that complicated. For the first four years of our business, my approach was as old school as you can get. I would simply gather business cards from people and staple them to a blank sheet of white copy paper. As I made calls and contacts, I would just document that on the white sheets of paper with a pen or pencil and keep them all in a file folder. Today I've gone a little high-tech, but not much. I track my pipeline on an Excel spreadsheet I've tricked and refer to as my Call Log. And I do like Trello for managing the flow of new clients and managing production projects. If you'd like a free copy of my call tracking log spreadsheet, please email me at info@govcon. win and I'll be happy to shoot that over to you.

If you're just starting out or you're not a tech savvy person, just staple business cards to white sheets of paper. I cleaned up with government contracting doing that. There's no reason that wouldn't work as well today as it worked 10-plus years ago. However you put it together for yourself, whatever the level of sophistication, just make sure at the end of the day you're doing it, and you're doing it consistently. Just do it.

The Wheel Keeps Turning

So now we've run through a full cycle of your Massive Action Plan. But that's just the first turn of the wheel. It doesn't stop there. In fact, that's just the beginning. You need to keep cycling through the steps as you learn and grow. You should be continuously updating your marketing plan based on everything you've experienced through the previous cycle.

The more times you make it around the track, guess what? Your branding and your profile credits increase. You become stronger. The more people you know, the more you grow. That sounds kind of cheesy, but still it's true. You've established a foundation for yourself, you're out there hitting the streets, calling on those federal prospects, going to the small business events. People are starting to know you, which is increasing your profile credit. Make it around the track as many times as you can. Everything gets easier and quicker the more laps you complete.

Today you might be spending 3 hours on social media, researching articles and ideas to post, and responding to the posts of others in your network. A year from now that same task may only take you an hour to complete. You'll find that you're going to have more to say and you're going to be able to say it quicker. You're going to be more efficient at building and adjusting your pipeline. You'll get better and faster at everything you do over time. So don't give up early in the process. Things get easier and faster the more you do them.

Your Marketing Battle Cry

Your marketing plan is your battle cry. What's your identity? Where are you taking this business? Where is it taking you? Your marketing plan is your guide, your roadmap to get you there. I have my battle cry posted on my laptop. I have it posted on the wall in my office. It's everywhere I am. Every time I see it I'm reminded of how I need to achieve the objectives I have for myself. I encourage you to do the same.

Adding Other Work to Your Pipeline

I know I have mentioned this previously, but it bears repeating. As I was going to association meetings, networking in person and doing social media, I found that other contractors were approaching me, saying things like, "Well, you know, we have a trade show, or we're moving into a new office space, we need new signage." And they'd ask me to perform these jobs for them. This was a personal growth life lesson at the time. I was overlooking dollars that were in front of my face within the community I was working in. I learned to say, "Hey, look. I am federally focused, yes, but I am available and open for business for government contractors because I speak your language."

I evolved my game to not leave dollars on the table. I'm not sure what type of business you're in but, if the government needs it, chances are larger government contractors or even small government contractors need your service as well.

Feedback Sources

How do you know what changes to make in your MAP and your marketing plan over time? Ask for feedback from everyone you're working with. Ask you staff about the type of work you're brining in and the clients you are serving. Are they the right projects and right clients to support your mission?

Ask end users, program managers and OSBDU folks how well you're fulfilling your contracts. How could you improve or enhance your offerings to support even more of their requirements? How do they feel about your capabilities statement? Does it accurately portray your company's identity to prospective federal buyers? Look for unsolicited feedback on social media and at networking events. What are people saying about you and your company? Have you done a good job establishing your profile and identity online and your reputation offline? If not, how can you improve? Plug those changes into your MAP and marketing plan on a continuous basis.

Chapter 10

Procurement Forecast

Wouldn't it be great if there were a free website where federal agencies would tell you what they intend to buy over the coming year, and what vehicles (small business designations) they intend to procure them through? And wouldn't it be awesome if there were a place where you could find the contact information of every small business office for every federal agency? No need to pinch yourself because you're not dreaming. Such a website does exist. It's called acquisition.gov.

Through acquisition.gov, you can locate the procurement forecast of every federal agency. You'll have to dig a little, but the links will take you to the individual agency websites, where you can see each agency's procurement forecast guides. You'll see what they intend to buy, what their budgeted price range is, and what vehicles they are planning to procure that service or product through, such as 8(a) or GSA, or HUBZone, etc.

The value of this website to you as a new federal contractor cannot be overstated. In addition to the forecasts, you'll have access to the contact information for all the contracting officers that handle the procurement. You can contact them directly to find further details regarding when the release is going to happen and anything else they are willing to share with you.

You can also look up all the OSDBUs and small business representatives within each of the agencies. Make those people a part of your call list for the day. Ask if they know of any upcoming requirements that match your NAICS codes or core competencies. Send them a PDF of your capability statement. Ask to schedule an in-person sit down meeting with them. When and if they give you 30 minutes of their time to present your capability statement, let them know you're not a newbie and start building a relationship. Make sure they understand that you're not there to get set up on fbo.gov. You're already fully set up, you have your capability and branding systems in place, and you're there to get down to business.

Ask them if they are familiar with your NAICS codes and core competencies. Who do they know within their agency that buys those products or services? They may be able to give you insight into what department might be looking to procure your services at some point in the future. What painting services, for example, might one of their departments have a requirement for towards fall of next year? Who is the program manager there? Can you give me their contact information? The more points of contact you have within a given agency, the more professional you look. The more you've done your branding, the more the OSDBU person is going to spend time with you because they see that you're serious and committed.

Be Prepared to be Misunderstood Initially

Even years after I had successfully built the branding for our business, as I'm teaching you to do, had held multiple prime contracts and was fully established to do federal work, I still often received an initial condescending response from some OSDBUs, who assumed I was a newbie when I first met them. But I don't take offense, it's only natural that they would assume that I was just like almost every other small business owner they speak to.

If a small business officer speaks to a hundred people every day, 97 of those 100 people are newbies who are not set up as I have shown you to do in this book. They haven't done the day-one work required. Just like anybody else, the OSDBUs are human. They're kind of on auto-pilot. They need to give that speech to 97% of the people. If you're a 3%er, you still might hear it just based on human habit.

Time is valuable, theirs and mine. They're only going to spend so much time with you so, you need to let them know early on that you have come to do business, not receive remedial mentoring. You might want to gently interrupt them early in the conversation to say something like, "You know, Mrs. Jones, I don't want to waste your time. I'm fully set up and I already do work with the federal government. I just want to do more work with your agency. I just want to get deeper in and be more of a service to your program managers." That statement allows you to cross an invisible line in their mind. They will snap out of it and say, "Oh, you're that 3%. Yes, we can get down to business."

That conversation will represent a bright spot in their day because they're tasked with finding small businesses that can perform services, allowing their agencies to meet their small business goals. Here is a viable candidate to help them meet those goals! Like anyone else, they get annual bonuses and other incentives based upon their performance. They're rated on how well they did meeting their small business objectives. Did they give 25% of the contracts to small business? Did they give 8% to women owned small business? All the agencies have small business goals. Be that person that's going to help someone achieve their goals.

What Procurement Forecasts Will Tell You

I recently pulled up two procurement forecasts on acquisition.gov, one for the Department of State and one for the General Services Administration (GSA). I was very quickly able to find all the requirement descriptions and the NAICS the agencies were looking to fill. I could also see the history of award category, such as 8(a), GSA, HUBZone or other designation they were targeting. I saw the agencies' budgets for the coming year, which they call an estimated value.

Within the procurement forecast you will also be able to find points of contact within the agency. You obviously don't want to call a point of contact in IT if you're doing painting. You want to look more for the construction side of things and then call that point of contact and say, "Look, I know you don't have anything listed for painting right now, but I see you do a lot of work with construction. Is there any construction requirement that you know of that I may be able to jump on?" Maybe there's a construction project that I may be able to latch onto with some teaming partners to do a take down and we can divvy up the labor accordingly from that point.

As always, add all relevant points of contact to your CRM or call log. Call them to find out when they'll have requirements that match your NAICS codes and core competencies. While speaking to one point of contact, be sure to always ask if they know of any other points of contact within the agency that you can call on directly to introduce yourself and let them know that you exist as a viable option in a particular area of expertise. You never know when they might lead you directly to your golden goose within that agency or department.

Chapter 11

Procurement Websites

In this chapter I'm going to share a number of websites where government contracting opportunities are advertised online. Just as I recommend that you spend time every day reaching out to OSDBUs and other contacts in federal agencies, you're going to want to spend an awful lot of time on fbo.gov and the other sites I'm about to cover. Procurement websites list live opportunities that can transform your business overnight.

First Step: SAM.gov

In order to sell to the U.S. Government, you must register with, and be approved by, the System for Award Management, found online at SAM.gov. There are a number of pieces of information you need in order to complete your application. This is a pretty lengthy process which involves answering a large number of questions including, "What's your D-U-N-S number?"

Before you can bid on government proposals, you need to obtain a Dun & Bradstreet, or D-U-N-S, Number, a unique nine-digit identification number for each physical location of your business. D-U-N-S

Number assignment is free for all businesses required to register with the federal government for contracts or grants. There is no cost for this service which is available at https://fedgov.dnb.com/webform.

In addition to your D-U-N-S number, SAM.gov is going to require information like your bank account number and routing number (so they can pay you via ACH). You're going to have to answer questions pertaining to your small business status, whether or not you or your business is a foreign entity, child labor laws, etc. They also have a bunch of FAR (Federal Acquisition Regulation) clauses and questions that they'll address through this registration process. They want to make sure there are no judgements against you, no outstanding warrants, you're current on your federal and state tax filings, etc.

Working the Procurement Websites

You're registered with SAM.gov. You've created your branding material and online profile. Your capabilities statement rocks the house. You're reaching out to your government contacts on a daily basis. It's now time to dig into the procurement websites to see what type of live opportunities are out there that you can start bidding on.

Here are a number of websites that I have my sales team look at daily. I said daily because they're fluid and ever-moving. While the government's always adding to them, you'll will see more activity toward the end of fiscal year, which is the last day of September. If a given agency does not spend all the money in their budget by the end of the fiscal year, they are in jeopardy of losing funds for the next year. So you're going to see more opportunities between July and September than you will the rest of the year. Nonetheless, you should always have your eye on the prize and go through these websites daily.

FBO.gov

The primary website for finding Federal Business Opportunities is FedBizOpps, also known as FBO. gov. All of the requirements over the value of $25,000 from every federal agency should be listed here, but you'll find that there are some that don't make it. You want to focus on the contracts and solicitations, as well as all the pre-solicitations and sources sought, which are where federal buyers are gathering information before they release a solicitation. You're looking for all the activity surrounding what it is you do. You can do searches based on keywords, NAICS codes, geography, a wide variety of different search options. You're going to want to spend a lot of time learning this site as you're first starting out.

You can set up a watch list on FBO.gov so that, every morning when you get in, you'll have an email of opportunities that meet the criteria that you've set up. As a more mature federal contracting business, we do get a lot of business from existing relationships and the BPAs (Blanket Purchase Agreements) we have in place. But we also get a lot of work that we bid on in the open market through FBO.gov.

GPO

GPO is the Government Printing Office, so it's more applicable to what I do. If you're not in a printing-related industry, then it may not be applicable to you.

https://contractorconnection.gpo.gov/

FedBid

FedBid is a private company that allows for reverse auction bidding like eBay. It's gotten a little tighter over the years. Eight or ten years ago, a lot fewer players were on it, and I used to win more lucrative contracts. But still, we do win some contracts off of it. If you win a job you find on FedBid, you will pay a percentage to them upon completion of the contract. So, there is a cost involved but there's no upfront money out of pocket.

http://www.fedbid.com/

FedConnect

FedConnect is a web portal that bridges the gap between government agencies and their vendor and grants applicant communities to streamline the process of doing business with government. There are a lot of Department of Interior jobs on FedConnect.

https://www.fedconnect.net/FedConnect/default. htm

GSA eBuy

The General Services Administration (GSA) serves as a procurement arm for the federal government. They manage government-owned buildings and also help agencies manage the process of procuring a variety of products and services. If you qualify, the GSA will assign you a schedule within your particular NAICS code, within your particular service code. As part of the process, you will have to negotiate discounted pricing with them on the products and services you provide.

The GSA Schedule is like a catalog federal buyers can use to find pre-approved vendors with products and services available at pre-negotiated prices. In other words, if the US Army wanted to buy a pallet of toilet paper, they could go to GSA and say, "Hey, we're looking for the most favorable pricing for a pallet of toilet paper." The GSA will have a schedule, a list of 90 vendors that sell toilet paper. All 90 players, all 90 vendors have negotiated most favorable cost pricing to the government. That's a very simplified explanation but I think it covers the concept pretty well.

If you have your GSA schedule, you can go on ebuy.gsa.gov and see where various agencies are looking for your product and service under your GSA schedule number, and then you get to bid on those contracts. The advantage of having your GSA Schedule is that you are one of a small pool of vendors listed for each NAICS code.

The last I checked, there were about 90 competitors that have the same GSA schedule I have. If something goes into GSA for bidding on eBuy, well, I've just reduced my competition from maybe 900 players out there on FBO or on FedBid, to 90 people. The disadvantage is that you will have pre-negotiated prices which you must honor, and which may be lower than what you may be charging agencies buying from you outside of the GSA Schedule.

I encourage you to look at getting your GSA schedule after you get established. I also encourage you to use a consultant to get your GSA schedule because it is a very time-intensive process. There are companies who will charge you up to $25,000 to get your GSA schedule. I think I paid about $3,500 to have mine done by a consultant out of Ohio. If you're interested in knowing that consultant's name, shoot me an email to info@govcon.win, and I'll share that person's contact information with you.

https://www.ebuy.gsa.gov/advantage/ebuy/start_page.do

FindRFP

FindRFP is a pay-for-use site that searches across the Internet and pulls information from a number of different sources like FBO.gov and even from state government procurement sites. FindRFP is a good site that I've used over the course of time.

http://findrfp.com/

NECO

NECO (Navy Electronic Commerce Online) is a procurement site run by the United States Navy. If the Navy buys what you sell, then you want to get set up with them.

https://www.neco.navy.mil/

Disclaimer

Some of these website links may have changed since I wrote this book. But, if you start with the main part of the URL, which is fedbid.com, or fedconnect.net, or findrfp.com, you'll be able to find what you're looking for.

Window Shopping

Some of these procurement sites require you to be pre-registered with SAM.gov and some will let anyone browse through the windows of opportunity. My recommendation is that you get yourself fully ready to bid on contracts before you start poking around to see what's available. Bite the bullet, dedicate a full day and get 'er done. It really sets you up for success.

The last thing you want to do is find a project that says the federal government's budgeting $100,000 in the Washington, DC area to buy XYZ, and you're like, "Wow, that's right in my wheelhouse!" But you're not registered on SAM.gov. You don't even have your D-U-N-S number yet. The DLA does a background check on all companies that register with SAM, so you have to wait for them for a few weeks. Before you know it, that $100,000 went to one of your competitors.

Building Momentum

It all comes back to that massive action plan. As you perform on that cycle, make laps around, the more you perform on prior federal contracts, the more your branding and profile get enhanced. Federal folks are risk-averse, so the more you show yourself to be a proven solution provider, the less risky you appear to procurement officers.

Rebidding Work You've Previously Performed

After you complete a given contract, you may or may not be a shoo-in to be selected the next time that agency needs to fill that requirement. It really depends on the goals of the agency and how you've performed. After you've performed on a contract, then you become the incumbent. If the contract was sole-sourced to you, if they're happy with you and you're still within budget, then there's a good chance that they'll come back to you as the incumbent and sole source that contract back to you. But there are a lot of times when you have to go out to bid against the contract that you just performed on.

How Many Contracts Should I Bid On?

New federal contractors may be concerned about landing more work than they can handle. My advice is to put in as many bids as you can, as long as they are all within your core competency and you're not stretching yourself too thin. No matter what, never bid on anything that you don't have the capability to perform on.

What if you bid on three bids, even though you only have the resources to perform on one, and you win all three? Then it's time to start looking at adding an industry partner. Add a teaming partner or vendor that can back you up with labor or materials. You can also go see your bank about securing a line of credit because you have these contracts in hand. If they give you the loan, use that capital to staff up or increase your resources, buy new machinery, etc.

Chapter 12

Capabilities Statement

It's critical that you have a well written and professionally designed one-page capability statement for your federal contracting business. This is your company's brochure for government buyers. Spend a lot of time crafting it and getting feedback from people on all sides of the table.

Wonder what a great capabilities statement looks like? Google "federal contractor capability statement" and review as many as you can find. Narrow down to two or three that you really like and use one or more of them as a template to share with a graphic designer to model after. Then plug in the text, graphics and contact information that support your marketing plan.

What Your Capability Statement Should Include

Your capability statement needs to contain all the branding and data necessary for a federal program manager, OSDBU person, end user or contracting officer to understand who you are, what you can do for them and why you are a safe choice when selecting a contractor to fill a given requirement.

Specifically, your capabilities statement should include:

- Your Company's Mission
- Core Competencies
- Competitive Differentiators
- Corporate Data and Contact Information
- CAGE and DUNS Numbers
- NAICS Codes
- Socio-Economic Factors (Designations)
- About Us

Your Mission Statement tells the federal buyer what is important to you and how you can help them succeed at their job.

Your list of Core Competencies lists the products and/or services you provide.

Differentiators show how you position yourself in the marketplace, what makes your offerings superior to, or different from, your competitors.

Your Corporate Data and Contact Information tell federal buyers where your office is located, how to contact you by phone or email, and how to find further information about you online.

You received a CAGE number when SAM.gov accepted your application to become a federal contractor. Buyers can use your CAGE number and your DUNS number to learn more about you and your past performance as a federal contractor.

Buyers are looking to match the NAICS codes of their requirements with the ones they find listed on your capability statement.

Socio-Economic Factors is another way of referring to designations. You should not only list your designations as text, but also include the associated logos. Make it clear in both words and graphics that your firm is a small business, a veteran owned business, a woman owned small business, and so forth. This information tells folks on the federal side, "Hey, if you want to get small business credit, I am a small business. If you'll award me this contract, which I am perfectly capable of performing on, you will also meet your small business goals."

Creating a strong capabilities statement that highlights your socio-economic factors generates a four-way win. The first win is that your small business gets the job. The second and third wins go to the contracting officer and small business officer because they have found a viable candidate to give the contract to. The fourth win is for the agency as a whole, because they're meeting their small business goals.

Every year, the heads of government agencies have to go before congress and ask for funding, and a question that they are often asked is, "How well are you meeting your small business targets?"

Senators and congressmen have to answer to their constituents, and small business owners are a very important constituency. Elected officials want to make sure that everything's not going to Lockheed Martin or BAE and the other big elephants. It's important that the government is buying as much as possible from small businesses because we are the economic engine for the country, providing millions of jobs to registered voters.

The About Us section adds a personal touch. You are not just about your core competencies and your business. There are real people driving that business, putting their hearts into what you're doing.

Professional Presentation

You've found one or more rocking capability statements online and had your graphic artist model yours after them. You've included all the sections I've listed here and put hours into writing the perfect text. You've distributed sample copies to friends on both sides of the contracting table and incorporated their feedback into your finished product. Now what?

Now you want to make sure that you present that masterpiece professionally every time it is requested, either online or in person. Have your artist generate two PDF versions of the finished product; one in high resolution for printing and one in low resolution for attaching to emails and downloading from your website. Send the high-resolution version to your local print shop and have it professionally printed on thick card stock, maybe even laminated. Make sure your capability statement is a grand slam, hitting on all the points, and screaming out to that contracting officer, "Take me seriously, I can do this work!"

Chapter 13

Proposal Generating System

Bidding on federal contracts costs you money, time and labor resources. You're going to find a lot of RFP activity, but not all of that activity matches you or your firm. With 11 million contracts awarded per year, there is an abundance of RFPs that you'll find as you're doing your daily digging and calling. There are going to be a lot of solicitations that are going to stretch you or fall completely outside of your target zone. I do museum exhibit work, so if I see an RFP for "Constructing a helicopter pad," I'm not going to bid on it.

You must have a bid/no-bid checklist for yourself with weighted scoring factors, so that you can quickly determine what RFPs you should be spending time on and which you should ignore, which ones you should put a bid out on and, more importantly, which you should resist the urge to put a bid on. How do you decide? Keep your core competency top-of-mind at all times.

Sticking to Your Knitting

Staying in your lane is going to be hard at first. You're going to want to bid on so much that you shouldn't. You'll see an RFP with requirements that at the margins of your core competencies and you'll say to yourself, "This requirement is number five out of our four core competencies, but I'm just dying to get into the game." Take a deep breath and just say no. There is no shortage of federal RFPs. It's an ongoing thing.

Uncle Sam will always spend a ton of money. The United States Federal Government will always be the world's largest buyer of goods and services. That next bid that's right for you, that's smack dab in the middle of your core competency, is right around the corner. You need to stay true to yourself, because if you start bidding on jobs that are outside your core competency, that's when you'll get burned. You lock in the contracts and then you're scrambling on the back end to figure out where you can find the expertise to actually perform on the job.

Just as you build your profile by getting your name out there, you can destroy your profile and reputation by not performing on contracts that you've been assigned. That's a surefire way of getting blacklisted with the federal government. You signed those contract awards when they came in, acknowledging that you meet the criteria and will perform successfully in a given timeframe. Contracting officers take it very seriously when you don't hold up your end of the bargain. Don't overextend yourself by bidding on RFPs that aren't directly in your wheelhouse. Be conscientious and stick within your core competency.

When you do decide to bid on a project, read the RFP very carefully and in full, because there will be a lot of verbiage in there, some of which could be detrimental to you. Buried in the middle of the RFP could be a requirement that the installer needs to be located within 20 miles of the facility, and that facility is in Portland, Oregon. Well, you're in Washington DC, and you don't have a full-time installer within 20 miles of Portland, Oregon. You're not in compliance with that RFP. If you submit a bid and are awarded the contract, you will find yourself scrambling to hire someone in Oregon – that you've never met before and know nothing about – to do the work for you.

The government's not doing that to trip you up. They're including that stipulation because they believe they're assembling the best set of requirements given the task that they need performed. Their belief that they need a local installer may be based upon what it's taken to get a favorable result on prior contracts that have been awarded.

Most of the time it makes sense to be sure you're complying with all the requirements. Occasionally however, you may want to call out a requirement that you feel is unnecessary to the successful performance of a contract. If you think that something that the contract states as mandatory is not critical, call it out in your response and say, "Look, I'm not meeting this requirement because I'm confident that I can perform on this contract at a competitive price without it. Please review my bid based upon that consideration." Just call it out there in a bold fashion.

You never know, they might not have good responses from other candidates, and they might make that concession with you. Just know that you're kind of putting yourself out on a limb, and it's very likely that they will eliminate you from consideration because you didn't meet that one stipulation. It could go either way.

Your Proposal Library

A key success factor for my company has been having a proposal library. We have a system of folder where we store the individual components of every proposal we have submitted. One folder contains our company overview, another has pictures of past performance, one has lists of points of contact for prior past performance. The folders are organized based on different response items that were requested previously so that, when a Request For Proposal comes in, responding to it is more of an assembly line process. We mechanically assemble the new proposal using parts and pieces of previous proposals. That allows us to put that proposal together and submit it in a timely fashion. As you can imagine, this is much more efficient than reinventing the wheel with a new intro letter, with a new company overview, with new pictures, every time you're responding to a new Request For Proposal.

A Note on Working with Subcontractors

Any time I'm taking on a sub, or even if I'm ordering a large supply of materials to perform on a job, I use a purchase order. In that purchase order I lay out all the terms of the transaction, what my expectations are, the price I'm willing to pay, down payment I'm paying, who the company is that I'm giving the sub work to or placing the order with. I also include a bunch of legal verbiage that protects me against possible non-performance by that subcontractor or vendor. Among other things, that language establishes the timeline that the other party is agreeing to adhere to. Hey, if that vendor says they're going to do it in eight weeks, well, they're going to have to sign their name to that. I won't use their services unless they sign my purchase order, which obligates them.

If they refuse to sign the purchase order, it's very unlikely that I will choose to do business with them. Their unwillingness to sign my purchase order tells me that they're non-committal. Sure, they'll cash my 50% check, they'll commit that way. But they're not going to commit in writing to what it is they've acknowledged verbally they're going to be providing. That makes me very uncomfortable. Always use a purchase order when subbing out work or ordering large supply from a vendor. Also get a certificate of insurance whereby they're adding the project name, and yourself as an additional insured to their policy. That's very important. You never know what's going on with someone else in their organization.

My vendors and subcontractors don't need to be registered with SAM or Dun & Bradstreet in order to support my federal contract work, they just need to be a credible company. I've worked with a lot of vendors over the years who didn't have either a CAGE number or a DUNS number, but were still very dependable and economically priced. I still have them sign a purchase order and provide the certificate of insurance.

Proposal Generation Flow of Activity

Here is a graphic which demonstrates the optimum structure you should set up within your company to generate proposals as quickly, efficiently and consistently as possible.

Proposal Generation Flow of Activity

Organizational Structure

First, you have organizational structure. Put some thought into having a full-time business development person (salesperson). Will you be having them doing this part-time in conjunction with commercial industry sales? Are you hiring someone specifically for federally-targeted business development? Are you doing it yourself? I did all of our federal business development myself for about five years before bringing on a sales team. Over the course of time I've pulled myself out of a lot of the activities, including sales.

Proposal Writer

I have a full-time proposal writer, which is a very significant investment as well as a tremendous asset to our company. Even if you have a proposal library in place and you're doing plug and play with different documents to craft a winning proposal, you still need a proposal writer to make all the final edits and adjustments. They are also committed to keeping the proposal schedule on track, and to making sure that they are being submitted on time.

If you submit a proposal one minute past the deadline, that contracting officer is technically supposed to reject your proposal, not even consider it. It's not like with commercial, work where a customer may tell you, "Hey, don't sweat it. End of the day will be fine." With federal work there's a specific time and date assigned to each proposal deadline. Adhering to it is the first step in showing your professionalism. What happens if you miss the deadline? The contracting officer is thinking, "Well heck, this guy can't even follow simple instructions with turn in the proposal on time. How am I going to trust him on a million-dollar contract?" The obviously answer is, he's not.

Estimator & Sales Manager

I do a lot of the estimating at our company myself. I kind of enjoy it. I have a good knowledge of the industry and material cost, so I make sure that the numbers are correct, and the margins are there. I do give a lot of estimating authority to our sales manager up to a certain dollar figure. But on larger projects I'll tend to do the estimating to make sure that we've caught all the detail points.

I don't ever want to put myself or my company in the situation where we're risking our survival because of some sloppiness. On lower-dollar proposals, I don't mind if we miss something here and there. There have been cases where I've missed some things, and we've taken down the job at a much larger profit margin than I had anticipated. I've had it go the other way too, where we got burned on a few deals over the years, barely breaking or even losing some money. I will not allow that to happen on larger dollar items, because I'm not prepared to take that hit.

Bid / No Bid Matrix

Create a customized matrix to help your team determine whether it makes sense to expend resources bidding on a given project. Your matrix is going to help you decide what the odds are of you being awarded a contract at a profitable price point. The matrix will give weighted emphasis to a variety of criteria within three primary areas of consideration:

1. Prospect Information
2. Internal Information
3. Market / Competitive Information

Prospect Information

Here you will be considering whether you know and/or can influence decisionmakers in that agency or department, if the budget has been formally approved and funded, are the requirements clearly defined and technically feasible, and a variety of other factors.

Internal Information

In this section of your decision matrix you will examine whether this opportunity is in synch with your own strategic direction, whether or not you have the resources, talent and will to win and perform the contract, and whether you have a successful track record with similar opportunities in the past.

Market / Competitive Information

Here you will consider whether you know who the competitive bidders are and whether they – or the incumbent – represent a significant threat, will winning the bid enhance your reputation and market positioning and give you an advantage over our competitors in the future.

That bid/no-bid document is going to evolve, as you change the requirements, criteria, and weighting system over the course of time. Nothing within your company should be stagnant. Everything should always be growing, progressing and improving.

Proposal Library

When you decide that you are going to bid on a given project, the RFP gets kicked down to the proposal manager working with the proposal library described earlier. Much of the verbiage found in the introduction letter, company overview, etc., stays the same. We just make minor tweaks. The capability statement, stays the same. But we almost always create customized technical response sections, so that way we're making sure that we're addressing all the points within the RFP.

The last thing you want to do is spend time sourcing an RFP and putting together a proposal, only to find that you didn't address a certain point that was required, and your bid got eliminated. I mean, how horrible is that? That's almost as bad as getting burned on a proposal because you missed something, got the job and lost money. All of that is in the same bucket of sloppiness.

I highlight the RFPs to make sure I catch all the points. That way, when the proposal writer is creating the proposal, they're catching all the points as well. It's one thing to lose a proposal because a competitor just really shaved down margins to get the job, to keep their guys busy. But it's another thing to lose a bid because you got disqualified for being sloppy. That's just doing yourself in. That's just wrong on all levels.

I have an estimate template in which I have all the labor categories hourly wages pre-filled, but which leaves the material section blank. I use it as a loose template for myself when I'm putting out a response. If the government client asks me to justify my numbers or wants itemized pricing, I have it right there.

I'll submit that along with my proposal to say, "Hey look, this requirement's going to entail a project manager, an account service manager, a graphic designer, a production manager, an install team, etc.," and just kind of lay it all out. There could be times when the government client didn't realize all those labor categories were needed to perform on this job, but now they understand, "Oh, this is why this company is presenting this higher price. They have a lot of past performance, so maybe they're someone we should listen to." That's kind of where you want to be at that level.

I don't want to talk too much about supporting your proposals with evidence of past performance because this book is geared towards folks who are just getting started winning prime federal contracts. Nonetheless, be aware that once you start building your past performance all of this gets easier. That past performance sells you in massive ways. Every time we submit a proposal, it includes a list of past performance which presents work we've done for the Secretary of Defense, the Secretary of the Navy, the Commandant of the Marine Corps, the Smithsonian Institution, the list goes on and on. If you take these steps presented in this book, you will quickly get to the point where you start building past performance, and then life gets a little easier.

General Colin Powell viewing our display cases in 2017

Exhibit for Air Force Headquarters

Exhibit cases for Lincoln's Courtroom at Fort McNair

Exhibit for Air Force Headquarters

Chapter 14

End of Fiscal Year

As mentioned previously, the last day of September marks the end of the fiscal year for federal agencies. They have to spend all the money within their budget before September 30 in order to justify needing that money for the following year. As a result, 77% of all the contracts we get every year are awarded to us between July and September. We call it the mad dash for cash.

Think about how significant that is for us in terms of workload, the amount of sourcing and proposals we're pumping out, the number of awards we're getting in. And then shortly thereafter, all the work we're starting on the contracts we've just won going into the fall, leading into the winter. This is a push that you and your team need to prepare for psychologically, and in terms of labor and resources.

Here are a few tips that help me get our company ready for end of every fiscal year.

Read the Entire RFP

There needs to always be an emphasis to read RFPs all the way through, including all the attachments and addenda. Everything has to be read, and all the critical points highlighted, even though you may be processing 5x to 10x the number of proposals during this period as you would the rest of the year.

Read through all that verbiage, dissect it and format it so your proposal writer can respond accordingly and avoid having the proposal eliminated from consideration because you missed some points. As always, during the bid/no bid process you want to make sure that proposal is within your core competency and that you fully understand all the requirements and can comply at a competitive price.

Researching the Procurement Websites

During this time your staff must comb through the procurement websites seven days a week. They can take turns regarding who works the weekends. At the end of the fiscal year, requirements come out daily, and that includes Saturday and Sunday.

Turnaround time for the submittals is also shortened drastically. Where you may normally have two weeks or more to respond to an RFP the rest of the year, you may only have a few days to respond during this period. You have less time to read through and analyze, which increases the odds that you may overlook something. Ignoring the procurement websites over the weekend can further shorten your turnaround time. If an RFP with a five-day deadline for response comes out on a Saturday, but you don't see until you come into work on Monday, you've lost 40% of the time you need to review and respond.

That goes hand in hand with limiting vacations and time off requests. I generally tell my team not to request vacation time in August and September, unless it's an emergency. This is when we're making our winters warm. If we're not hitting it with all we have seven days a week during August to September, well we're going to have a cold winter. Everything works off lag, so whatever we do today will affect us six months to a year down the road. That especially holds true with government work because things are stretched out more than in the commercial world.

In commercial work, you can get a contract today and be hitting the ground running tomorrow. In federal contracting, you get a contract today and the kick off meeting may not happen for 30 or 60 days. And that's just the kick off. The actual work may not commence until many weeks later. Ensure that during July, August and September you're making a full, concerted effort to contact everyone on your call log and in your CRM database.

You never know when money will get filtered to a department that you have a relationship with. An unannounced requirement could pop up. Some higher-up official wants a new display outside their office, and there is money left in the budget that needs to be spent immediately. That requirement may have been on the back burner the day prior but, since it's end of fiscal year and some money freed up, well now it's priority A. That's when you want to be top-of-mind with that small business rep or that program manager. And you need to be ready to roll with the proposal response in a timely fashion, so that way you can put yourself on a good footing to win that work.

End of Fiscal Year Partnering Opportunities

In the commercial space, competitors are usually your antagonists. I mean, they're people that work against you, they're trying to win the same work you're trying to win. But, in the federal government, sometimes they can be your allies, especially during end of fiscal year. Remember that scenario I gave before where one of your federal competitors in California won a project that had a requirement for install work in Washington, DC? Well, you can contact that California company and offer your installation services, and it may be more advantageous, more cost beneficial for that company to use you for installation services, knowing that you're fully vetted to do work with the government, knowing that they don't have to travel and put their folks on the road at a time when they may be very busy.

Hurry Up and Wait

It bears repeating that, even though your federal buyers are going to be in a hurry to award contracts at the end of fiscal year, you may not see any revenue for a year or more after landing a bid.

Some contracts begin engagement almost immediately and begin paying much sooner, but they are the exception rather than the rule. They are usually staffing requirements I call "butts in seats" contracts. A government agency will need five IT folks to go to work immediately on a given project. The agency contracts with an IT staffing firm to provide five workers to begin working full-time at a government office. They start immediately, and the staffing firm will begin receiving payments within thirty days.

My projects don't work that way. Most of my awards are firm, fixed-price contracts. Upon my delivery of the finished project and a satisfactory inspection of my work by the project manager, he or she will submit the receiving report to the contract officer. I can generally expect to receive payment within 30 days after that happens.

But that's not 30 days after I received the award. I don't generally perform fully on a contract for six months to one year after I receive the contract. And then, 30 days after that six to twelve-month period, I get paid. Add another month for the period of time between when we first bid and were awarded the job and you could be looking at twelve to eighteen months before you get paid on a project you've bid on. That's a very daunting prospect for someone who is new to federal contracting and it is one of the biggest obstacles business owners cite when describing why they choose to avoid this arena.

Here's the thing though, once you cross that initial hurdle, you're always going to have cash flow, because you're always going to have projects in the pipeline Once you start closing out contracts, you'll be bringing in new contracts in for the next year. After that first year to eighteen months, you'll never again feel that burn.

Government work is much more lucrative because it's consistent and they buy at a much higher scale than do commercial or consumer-level customers. Let's say you provide a service for homeowners and you've just finished a great $1,000 job for a new customer. You hope that customer will call you again later but there's no guarantee they will. You hope they will refer you to their friends and neighbors, but they probably won't. There's a lot of mystery surrounding where you next job is going to come from.

You have much more control on the government side. I've shown you how to determine which agencies buy the most of your product or service. You know who they're currently buying from and how much they're paying. When you land a job it's much more likely to be for $100,000 than $1,000. And, using the techniques you're learning here, you can create a continuous pipeline of orders from the world's largest buyer who pays within thirty days, every time. I wouldn't trade it for the world.

Find a way to make it through that year or so and get to where you have cashflow you can count on going forward. Only 5% of small businesses are doing business with the federal government. Figure out how to become a member of that elite class. It will change your business, and your life, dramatically.

Chapter 15

Looking to Team?

Are you considering teaming with other federal contractors to win bids and generate revenue you think you couldn't achieve on your own? Proceed with caution. I intentionally put a question mark in the title of this chapter to highlight how important it is to be careful who you team with.

Prime Contractor vs. Subcontractor

The first thing I want to make clear is the difference between a prime contractor and a subcontractor in the federal space. The prime contractor is the organization that has a direct contract with the federal government to provide goods or services. A subcontractor is a vendor that works for the prime contractor as the prime contractor is satisfying the requirements of their contract with the federal government. The sub works for the prime and the prime works for the government.

Who Is Your Potential Teaming Partner?

Over time, you will encounter potential opportunities to team. When that happens, and you have a potential partner in mind, the first question you need to ask is how well you know that teaming partner. Have you worked with them before? Do you know the owner? What is their location? Have they done work with the federal government before? These factors will give you some insight into whether they are going to make you look good or make you look bad while helping you perform on a contract.

Who Controls the Federal Buyer Relationship?

The next question you need to ask is, "whose client is it?" If you're targeting an opportunity which will require you to bring on a teaming partner, will the federal buyer be your client or theirs? Have either of you sold to that agency previously? Is it nobody's client? Perhaps neither of you have a past track record with this agency but you see an opportunity on FBO that will require your two firms to team to bid on, win and perform.

The question of "whose client is it?" is a very important one to answer because it will determine who the prime contractor is and who the subcontractor is. If the agency is your client, then you're going to want to set things up to ensure you're protecting that client relationship going forward. This especially holds true if you don't know your teaming partner very well. They could move in on the territory and undercut you. You want to make sure that you have protections in place.

Make sure that you're using legal counsel to draft all of your teaming agreements. Hire an attorney that's well versed in government contracting. Your teaming agreement needs to be much more than just a simple, "Jason's going to do haul away and Fred's going to patch and paint on the way out." There's a contract between you and the agency. There's an RFP with a bunch of FAR clauses that must be understood and adhered to. And there may be small business requirements that say Fred is a large company and this is a small business set aside, so 51% of the work needs to be done by Jason. The attorney will not know or understand all those important details unless they are well versed in government contracting and they have access to that RFP. A good federal contracting attorney will study all the documents to make sure that your teaming arrangement is not only fair and equitable, but it's also in compliance with the federal requirements.

Teaming with Large Companies

Be extremely cautious when partnering with large companies. They can be brutally competitive and may take you out of the relationship with no recourse. They will always want to use their teaming agreement because their legal counsel wrote and approved it. They are big and experienced and will attempt to steamroll you by controlling the process. "Here's the agreement, we will not concede any points, take it or leave it." Even if you're in the prime seat and the big company is your sub, you have obligations as a prime contractor to do a certain percentage of the work. The government's not giving you the contract so you can have a large company do all the work and then you just charge a 10% fee. Everybody will get in trouble and you'll get blacklisted.

There's no point in being the prime contractor if you're just going to be a pass-through person, having the large companies do all the work while you take your cut and be on your way. As appealing as that may sound, because you're not putting the effort in, you will be out of compliance with the federal contract. You're risking future federal work and you're probably giving that client away to the large company. There's no win-win in any of that. Whatever the case, make sure that you're protected by having everything clearly defined in the partnering agreement, and have your own lawyer read over the big company's document.

Is Teaming Really the Solution?

When considering an opportunity that will require a teaming partner, look at what problems you feel would be solved by teaming. How can a teaming arrangement solve that problem and how will you and the teaming partner fit together? Who's doing what and at what time? How will accounts receivable work? Will you pay that partner within ten days of receiving payment yourself? Do you believe there is true synergy with the both of you connecting and joint-venturing on this opportunity? These are some of the initial questions to ask yourself.

MAP Now, Team Later

If you can avoid teaming while you're getting started, do so. It could muddy the waters and potentially veer you off course. I strongly suggest spending the first year just working within that massive action plan. Take all those laps with your marketing plan, your profile, your branding, social media and associations, your small business events. Build your pipeline and repeat, repeat, repeat.

Spend the first year doing that before entertaining the idea of adding teaming partners. I would also wait that first year before going out for your small business designations or GSA schedule. You'll get all those things faster when you can show past performance to the agencies that issue those designations.

As a general business practice, I've done very little teaming over the years. Sometimes, on larger projects that we've brought in, I have had a vendor do more of the work on the backend. Maybe if it's a project that it involves a lot of assembly work, I may have them do more of the fabrication and assembly at their plant and then send it over to me where we'll do the finishing and installation. I may lose a little bit more money doing it that way, but I'm able to perform on the contract and am still getting the margins that I forecasted. The more contracts I am able to fulfill successfully, the more goodwill and branding I'm generating among federal buyers.

No matter what, don't lose your identity through partnering. A potential partner may approach you with what sounds like a panacea, "Hey let's team. Let's go after this. Let's do some co-branding efforts. Let's merge our logos, submit joint proposals." Don't do it. That will only distract your focus from making your daily calls, looking at the procurement websites, going through the procurement forecasts, looking at USAspending.gov for competitor information, and all the other tasks you know you must consistently perform in order to succeed as a prime federal contractor. Focus on the daily grind and work that massive action plan. That will get you to where you want to be.

Chapter 16

Small Business Designations

In this chapter we're going to cover small business designations, programs the government uses to funnel as much spending to small businesses as possible. One of the best places to learn more about designations is the Small Business Administration's SBA.gov website.

https://www.sba.gov/contracting/government-contracting-programs

The link above takes you to a page which gives an overview of small business government contracting opportunities. That link was current and correct at the time of printing but, as always, it may have changed by the time you're reading this. You can always start on the SBA.gov website, and then look up government contracting programs, which is probably only a click or two away.

Are You Ready for This Step?

I don't recommend that you research or pursue any designations right out of the gate, because that may serve as a distraction as you're working through the massive action plan. But it should be something that is in your plan, your future plans, with government contracting. As I stated in the previous chapter, maybe after the one-year point you can start looking at securing designations.

What Are Designations?

Many agencies will have a goal to award at least 25% of their contracts to small businesses. When it comes to contracting products and designations, such as woman-owned, veteran-owned, etc., they may have certain contracts set aside for these designations to help them achieve their goals. The intention of this chapter is not to drill down into each one of these designations. I just want to give you a general overview, so you know that these designations exist, and that you can leverage them to obtain contracts and further your growth with federal contracting.

Hub Zones

A hub zone is a socio-economically disadvantaged location where both your company and a certain percentage of your employees must reside. If you go to the hub zone program link, you'll see a map that shows you the different hub zone areas across the country.

Woman-Owned Small Business

The woman-owned small business designation requires that at least 51% of the company is owned by one or more women, and that the company meets the size criteria to qualify as a small business.

Veteran-Owned or Service Disabled Veteran-Owned Business

These two designations are certified by the Department of Veteran Affairs. All honorably discharged veterans are eligible for veteran-owned designation, but only veterans who have been certified as service-disabled are eligible for the service disabled veteran-owned designation.

8(a) Business Development Program

The 8(a) Business Development Program is designed to support socioeconomically disadvantaged persons. It's not just a program for minority individuals that live in the US. There are also other characteristics, and other types of individuals, that can qualify for that program. Click on the link for 8(a) business to see if you'd qualify.

Small Disadvantaged Business

Small disadvantaged business is a self-certified designation where you say that you're not only a small business, but you're also disadvantaged in some respect. Go through the qualifications on the site to learn whether you may qualify.

GSA Schedule

The GSA schedule is a federal supply schedule for IDIQ contracts, indefinite delivery indefinite quantity, long-term contracts. Many government contractors get their GSA schedule, because it really opens you up to a lot of contracts that aren't listed on FBO.gov. It's just a whole new avenue through which you can sell to the federal government.

https://www.gsaelibrary.gsa.gov/ElibMain/home.do

The link above takes you to the GSA eLibrary, where you can do a quick search and find which contract is applicable to the type of product or service that you provide. On that page is a link called "View Schedule Contracts," which will allow you to search for one that is applicable to you. Oftentimes there may be a few schedules that you would qualify for, or that would fit within your core competency. If that is the case, when you file for your GSA schedule, you may want to file for several schedules. File for all the schedules that fit within your core competency.

When you click on the "View Schedule Contracts" link, it will also give you information on all your competitors that hold this schedule. It lets you know who's in the game with you. You should recognize a lot of those names and faces from USASpending.gov because, as you immerse yourself into the federal contracting world, you'll see a lot of names and faces repeat themselves. That's when you know that you are gaining traction with the work you've done so far.

How to Sell Through GSA

The link below takes you to a page on the GSA website that offers some really helpful tips on how to increase sales through GSA.

https://www.gsa.gov/acquisition/new-to-gsa-acquisitions/how-to-sell-to-the-government

Getting a GSA Schedule

Again, I used a consulting firm to file and obtain my GSA contract. I was very happy with them, and they were very affordable and effective. If you email me at info@govcon.win, I will send you the consultant's name. I'm not vouching for them, but I'm telling you I had a good experience.

GSA Advantage

If you get your GSA Schedule, you will be given the opportunity to join GSA Advantage, an online shopping site where you can promote your products to government buyers, just as you might to consumer and commercial buyers on Amazon or eBay.

Tying It All Together

I hope you're picking up on the theme here: The more you get your name out there, through designations, the GSA schedule, GSA Advantage, etc., the more money you're going to make. The more contracts you're going to knock down. It's all about exposure. If nobody knows you, nobody is going to give you any contracts. Nobody knows how to give you money. It's as simple as that.

Get known through as many channels as you can, and you will find that government clients will be attracted to you, instead of you always having to pound the pavement to source new business.

Chapter 17

Wrapping Up

Thank you so much for investing your time and attention into reading this book. Before I sign off, I want to share some final thoughts and resources with you.

Leaders Are Readers

You should continue to read books on the subject of government contracting and become a lifelong student of the industry. The vocabulary that you'll gain from reading these books will help you as you're building your brand, as you're building your profile, and as you're connecting with government clients. It will equate to more dollars in the door, not just more knowledge in your head.

Government Contracts Made Easier, by Judy Bradt

Government Contracts Made Easier is loaded with resources that seasoned contractors take years to discover, including: Key Concepts, Profiles in Success, A Ten-Step Structured Approach to Winning Government Contracts, Exercises, Research Data, Top Expert Insights, Checklists and Tip Lists.

Available on Amazon: http://amzn.to/2CPQjvE

Selling to the Government, Mark Amtower

While anyone can play in this market, only those with the right preparation can win. Selling to the Government offers real-world advice for successful entry into the biggest market anywhere. Get proven approaches, strategies, tactics, and tools to make your business stand out, build relationships, understand procedures, and win high-stakes contracts.

Available on Amazon: http://amzn.to/2FHf0xl

Zero to A Billion, David Kriegman

Zero to a Billion is an insightful, practical, how-to guide for entrepreneurs who want to build a successful government contracting business, written by an experienced and respected expert in the field. Kriegman draws on his thirty years of experience to illustrate the essential lessons of strategy, business development, cultural issues and operations with real-world examples and actionable ideas.

Available on Amazon: http://amzn.to/2GTajzI

80/20 Sales and Marketing, by Perry Marshall

In this wonderful book, Perry Marshall applies the 80/20 rule to sales and marketing and proves that 80% of your revenue comes from 20% of your clients. While this book is not about government contracting specifically, the lessons it teaches apply to all businesses and virtually every aspect of life.

When you're doing work with the federal government you need to identify who your most profitable clients are. But that's just the beginning. After you find that 20% of your clients who are bringing you 80% of your profits, you need to apply the 80/20 rule again to find the 4% who are bringing you 64% of your earnings. A third application will reveal the 1% of your clients who are generating 50% of your profits.

Available on Amazon: http://amzn.to/2F3RfCi

Thank you so much for entrusting your time and money into purchasing and reading this book. Learning these tricks of the trade is going to give you a huge head start in your quest to begin acquiring prime federal contracts. I haven't left anything out. Everything that I have shared here are all the same things I've done to grow our business out of the basement of our home and into a large commercial fabrication and warehouse facility.

The best business decision we made was developing and maintaining a focus on prime federal contracts. Along the way we have met a lot of small businesses that just went for the lower hanging commercial fruit or went to work on a sublevel for some major prime organization. None of them have enjoyed the growth and profitability that our company has been blessed with.

Even with this book as your guide, you may wish to have someone helping you on a more direct, personalized level. Send me an email if you have any interest in mentorship. I offer a six-month mentor/protegee program on a very limited basis. I can only take on a few folks at a time. Email me at info@govcon.win and put Mentorship Program in the subject line. I'll reply with the details of the program.

Thank you again for joining me and God bless.

Korean War Exhibit fabricated and installed for the Pentagon to commemorate the 60th Anniversary of the Korean War

Afterword

Subsequent to the completion of the production of Martin Saenz online video course, Secrets to Winning Government Contracts, Powerhouse Publishing's Frank Felker sat down with Martin to ask him some additional questions on the content. After reviewing that interview, Martin asked to have it included in this book. What follows is an edited transcription of their conversation.

Frank Felker:

Glad to have you here Martin. Regarding your online course, *Secrets to Winning Government Contracts*, I've actually gone through the course twice, and I'm seeing things, hearing things, learning things, that I missed the first go-round. I want to congratulate on providing such a complete information resource, but still, I've got a few questions that I would like to ask you. I want to ask these questions from the perspective of a dear friend of mine, who has a small federal contracting business that provides training services, primarily to the Department of Defense. So, for the reader of this Afterword, I want to make clear that this is the perspective from which I'll be asking the following questions.

Introduction and Strategy Overview

Let's get started with the first chapter of your book, which is not so much about federal contracting as it is about the business owners themselves, their own personal goals, their goals for their company, and their mission statement. I think a lot of people might be surprised that you start with that. Why do you feel that getting clear about your personal why is the most important place to start?

Martin Saenz:

Business is always personal. Whatever you choose to do in business is always going to come from the perspective of what's in your comfort zone. If you have an HVAC company, and you sell heating and air conditioning units to consumers because that's who you feel comfortable speaking to and working with, then that's probably how you're going to grow your business from a sales and service perspective. If you're someone that just likes to deal with business owners, or large property facilities, then you'll probably bypass consumers and go straight in marketing to other business owners, business savvy type people. When you consider selling to the federal government, it is a massive commitment. And with any kind of massive commitment, you should always start with what is the why. Do I have the mental stamina that will allow me to put in the effort, to put in the physical resources, to accomplish becoming a successful federal contractor?

So, everything starts with goals, with goal setting. You're not only preparing yourself mentally to do the work at the given time, you're also starting with the end in mind, envisioning where you want to end up as a federal contractor. A lot of times you'll find that companies who are doing, two, three or four hundred thousand dollars a year in gross revenue selling to consumers or other businesses, are looking for the larger long-term contracts that the federal government can offer. However, in order to get there, you need to have your mind right from the beginning. Get clear on your why from the start.

Frank Felker:

And are you saying that getting clear on your why will help you get through the tough spots and do what it takes in order to get through that initial 12 months where you may not see any revenue come in from your efforts targeting the federal government?

Martin Saenz:

It's that, plus a lot more. Getting clear on your why will help you get through the hard times, but moreover it's going to help you have the will to get started in the first place. Everybody talks about goal setting all day long. Experts will tell you that you need to visualize, meditate and have the right rituals in place to form good habits. Everybody talks about that, but then 95% of the people drop off when it comes to actually taking action. So, this initial goal setting helps lead you towards building a successful marketing plan that you're going to put into action.

Frank Felker:

Another thought that comes up in that very first section is the general level of risk aversion among federal buyers. As you know Martin, marketing is my business. And, being a Washington, DC-based marketing guy for my entire career, for years people have approached me and asked, "Can you help me market to the federal government?" To which I always have always replied, "Absolutely not. That's a total mystery to me." Now, thank goodness, you've helped make it clearer to me. One of the biggest mysteries you cleared up for me was the mindset of the federal buyer and the culture they operate within. Please speak to the culture that you need to be aware of and become a part of, as you begin to contract with the government.

Martin Saenz:

You need to have a great deal of patience, finesse, and persistency. At the end of the day, even though you're selling to the federal government, you're still selling to people. There are still people on the other side of the table, and a lot of those people in the federal government are very skeptical. They've been burned by vendors in the past; contracts that they've issued, where the contractor didn't know what they were bidding, fell through on the project, or went belly up midway through. That's the last thing that government employee or contractor wants to have happen, because it reflects poorly on them.

Just like any other person out there, they want to do a good job for themselves and their agency. They want their good work to reflect well on their boss and their boss's bosses, on up the chain. When it's time for their bonuses, when they're due for raises and promotions and so forth, they want to receive positive reviews. It's really just about understanding that human element.

Each individual agency also has its own personality that you need to reflect in your personality when you're dealing with them. When I'm talking to someone at Smithsonian, whether it's OSDBU (Office of Small Disadvantage Business Utilization) or a contracting officer or a program manager who's a curator at one of the museums, I know that it's a more art-centric environment. When I'm building exhibits for the Smithsonian, creativity's going to be extremely important, the types of materials that I'm going to be using, and so forth. A person I'm dealing with there may be more inclined to be more liberal in their thinking, not necessarily politically, just kind of that free-thinking mentality. You're going to find that type of person at the Smithsonian Institution.

On the other hand, if I'm talking to high levels within the Department of Defense, then it's going to be a little more rigid, and it's going to be more about the impact of the exhibit that I'm going to create and build. They're not necessarily going to care as much about the materials or how the layout's going to take place. Knowing your audience, and that each agency has its own type of culture, is extremely important to succeed in this arena.

Core Competencies:

In Chapter 3 you talk about core competencies. Your recommendation is to stick with four or fewer core competencies. I want frame my question to you about this from the perspective of my friend's training business. The number one course they offer teaches federal acquisition law to people who procure goods and services for the government. Federal acquisition law training to contracting officers is an extremely narrow area of focus. "Training" can cover a lot of ground, from avoiding sexual harassment behavior to dealing with a multi-generational workforce. Recently a request for proposal came into her company for some leadership training, which is way out of their core competency. If training is as wide as the ocean, and federal acquisition law training is as narrow as a pinpoint, how broad or narrow should you go? It seems like a tough question.

Martin Saenz:

Look at things like the rings of a tree. If you cut down a tree and look at the rings, starting from the center on out, you can determine its age. If I were your friend, I would start with that pinpoint focus on federal acquisition law, and then try to see what's just beyond that. Maybe general contract law, the Federal Acquisition Regulation, FAR clauses, things like that. And then what's after that? It may be small business, as it relates to contracts, as it relates to meeting small business goals and objectives that each agency has. Then expand it out, take baby steps outward until you get to that level where you feel like you're dropping off, expertise-wise.

Competitive Intelligence:

Chapter 4 has to do with competitive intelligence. It was such an amazing revelation that you shared about usaspending.gov, and the federal procurement data system. All this free information is available online about all the contracts that have been let, who won them, how much the government paid, etc. I shared that site with my friend in the training business and, after reviewing it, she said, "I went to that usaspending.gov, but it doesn't tell me what contracts are coming out, it only tells me what happened before." What would your response be to her reaction? What's the real value that you can get from studying those websites?

Martin Saenz:

Well, I think two things. For one, you understand the agencies and departments that are procuring what it is you sell. Number two, you see who the big fish are in your industry, so you can begin modeling after their success from a marketing standpoint. Look up your competitors websites. Any company that it sells on a high level to the federal government will have their website designed to speak to that federal contracting officer. It gives all the NAICS codes, your CAGE code, your Dun & Bradstreet number. It gives the verbiage that the government client wants to see, and it gives testimonials and case studies. Government folks love to see case studies. It lists past performance, which is on most requirements. Go to usaspending.gov to identify your competitors and then visit their websites to get ideas on how to redefine your messaging and enhance your image.

The cherry on top is that you can do outreach to those top competitors for teaming partnerships. If you have a large competitors based out of Denver, Colorado, and you find that they just won a contract in Washington DC, well you might be able to help them. If you're located in Washington DC, and can perform the work, they may choose to have you do some or all of it.

The last thing I will say is that you're an average of the five people you associate with. Get in the habit of associating with your five most successful competitors. You will grow as a result.

Massive Action Plan (MAP):

Chapter 5 talks about your concept of the massive action plan. The MAP you describe starts with your marketing plan, and then moves on to building what you were just talking about, your profile and reputation online, participation with government contracting associations, attending small business events and building your pipeline with all the connections you're making through the other steps. In this chapter you also talk about Guerrilla Marketing. You read Jay Conrad Levinson's book and apparently it really spoke to you. You say that we should have a really short, one-page guerrilla marketing plan. Can you speak to that for a minute, because when people start to write a business plan or a marketing plan, they think it's got to be as thick as the phone book.

Martin Saenz:

You should simplify everything in your life. The massive action plan, when successfully applied to selling to the federal government, requires a ton of effort. It could be called the massive effort plan, because that's what it requires. Look at all the steps involved; you're branding your image, you're building your profile through social media, you're joining associations. You're not just joining associations, you're joining, and on an ongoing basis, you're participating. You're continually doing competitive intelligence through usaspending.gov. Everything is on an ongoing basis, so the more you can simplify each step, the more success you're going to have within those steps. That's just the simple fact of life. Some people start federal contracting working with some fancy consultant who either has never sold to the federal government or, if they did, they worked for a huge company. They never built a federal contracting business of their own from scratch. But now they have a training outfit or and they promise you the world.

So you go and you buy their book, you attend their program, and you do a few activities, and then you drop off the map. You get back into your day-to-day grind of selling to the consumer, of selling to small businesses or large companies. You never achieve sustained growth in the federal arena. The ideas behind guerrilla marketing is to simplify your marketing plan so that you can not only create it on the onset, but then you can keep it a living document, that you look at on a daily basis, as you're moving through each phase of the massive action plan.

Profile and Reputation:

In Chapter 6 you talk about your profile, your LinkedIn profile, and your reputation within the industry. This is in alignment with what I'm accustomed to in commercial and consumer-facing marketing, which is that your messaging, your colors, your branding, everything needs to be consistent, from your website to your LinkedIn profile, to your print collateral material. I would have thought that government buyers could not care less about that kind of thing. Why is this so important for federal contractors?

Martin Saenz:

Federal buyers are very risk averse. They're not looking to take many chances with you. Before they give you a contracting opportunity, for that matter, before they're even going to spend five minutes talking to you about an opportunity, they need to have some comfort level that they're not wasting their time. They will go to your website, they will look over your capabilities statement, they will look at your business card thoroughly, before giving you a contract. I've heard that feedback from contracting officers time and time again. They are watching all your steps, and they're seeing if you're someone that is a professional. If you spend the time that is required to get the little things right, then chances are you're going to spend time on the big things that count, and that's performance on the contract.

That's why it's critically important that you have your branding down, that everything is consistent. And that all needs to be done before you hit the street on social media, before you go to the associations, before you start reaching out to those five people that you want to be the average of. Those people are also going to be vetting you too, based on your appearance through branding and marketing.

Associations and Social Media:

Chapter 7 talks about participation in federal contracting associations. I began researching associations that might be appropriate for my friend's training business, and I found AFCEA. They apparently are a huge association with a lot of regional offices. They do a lot of events. But the underlying name of the acronym is "Armed Forces Communication and Electronics Association". She doesn't have any connection to electronics, but she does target the Department of Defense. Would this association be good for her to get involved with?

Martin Saenz:

Yes, absolutely. It's DoD focused. It's a large and robust organization. It's well run. But, like anything else, it's not about whether it's a good organization for her to get involved with, it's about will she have the time commitment to go to all the events, to become a sponsor within AFCEA, to work and volunteer and be on boards and in charge of association activities? AFCEA's a great organization, and if you are going to put the time and resources and commitment into joining and actively participating in an association, then you should choose a sound, established one like AFCEA.

Small Business Events:

Now, speaking of her time investment, Chapter 8 has to do with agency small business events, also known as industry days. Being that she's located in the Washington DC area, I'm sure there is no shortage of small business base events that she could attend. What do you think is a sensible number for her to set as a goal to attend, let's say, in a month's time?

Martin Saenz:

It's not so much the quantity, but the quality. She should only attend industry days that will maximize the return on her time investment. Here's how industry days get set up: The program managers let the contracting officer know, "Hey, we're going to have a requirement in this field, in this category." The contracting officer collects a bunch of different upcoming requirements from one or more program managers in his agency or department. The contracting officer needs to be sure that there will be enough suitable vendors in those categories, to perform on those contracts. So they put out an industry day event notice.

As a federal contractor, the first thing you need to do after receiving the notice is to call the person who's running the industry day to learn whether they're looking for goods and services that you provide – or something complementary – during that event. Maybe they don't have training needs in your exact contract area, but they just might have training needs for other human resource requirements. If so, your friend might want to attend just to get in front of the same person that might specify a need for her service later.

It's a vetting process. You need to vet each and every industry day. Based on the responses you get from the contracting officer or the event planner, you'll know whether that's one you need to attend. Whether you attend one industry event a year or ten a year, the important thing is that everyone you attend it is worthy of your time investment. I won't hesitate to travel to St. Louis to attend an industry day if I'm confident that they have a serious requirement for work I perform. But I won't drive down the street if it's going to be an industry day event on IT. That would be a waste of my time.

Building Your Pipeline:

In Chapter 9 you talk about the last step in the massive action plan, building your pipeline, filling your pipeline with contacts, opportunities and jobs. Again, this is something which is in direct alignment with what I'm accustomed to in the commercial sales and marketing world. You meet people at industry days, at association events and online, you gather their contact information and put it into your CRM. Then, as you called it, you start smiling and dialing to keep yourself front-of-mind with them, Is there any aspect of the filling your federal pipeline that you would say is starkly different from the commercial world?

Martin Saenz:

Yes, everything is long term in the federal government. You could be talking to a contracting officer or program manager in January, not see the requirements until August, bid on it in

August, win it, and then not start performing until December. That's a one-year time period. Commercial contractors generally don't think in terms of that length of time. You show up at the door of a small business and say, "Here's the estimate. When do we get started?" And the client is like, "Okay, here's a credit card, let's get rolling." When you first start working in the federal arena, a lot of what you feel like might be wasted time, initially will pay dividends down the road, if you just stay with it. Another important point is that the federal employee is not interested in doing any wheeling and dealing. They're not looking for back and forth negotiations or communication. It's very regimented, very by the book.

When you talk to them, it's always more of just a pleasant encounter. "Oh, Mr. Jones, I just wanted to reconnect, let you know that we're still out here breathing. I'm going to resend you my capability statement, just in case you don't have a copy. I know that you know to call me when something does pop up." It's a very pleasant thing with no pressure or hard sell. But if I'm talking to a property manager on the commercial side, then I'm like, "You know what, just give us a chance, you'll see. We'll show up at your doorstep tomorrow. We'll survey the job site. I'll have a price for you by end of week." Talking to a government employee requires a lot more finesse. It's a longer-term game so you need to have patience.

But what you don't want to do is just sit there twiddling your thumbs. You need to be moving on building your castle one sand pebble at a time. Get the next Mr. Jones on the phone and let him know, "Mr. Jones Number Two? Just want to let you know, we're still out here breathing." And then the third Mr. Jones, and the fourth Mr. Jones. You're building a database of large numbers of people, each receiving consistent, very gentle taps with and the hope that they'll remember you when have a requirement that fits you.

"Hey, that nice fella, that can do what I need done, just called me again. Let me go punch up his website." They punch up the website. "Wow, he looks professional. Look at his past performance! He's done work for the Secretary of Defense, General Colin Powell, Secretary of the Navy, Commandant of the Marine Corps, a whole host of work, all around the Pentagon. Wow! He's a nice fella *and* he knows what the heck he's doing. If he can perform successfully for all those folks, he can sure as heck do work for me."

Frank Felker:

A commercial sales person feels the pressure to try to persuade someone to take action immediately. But here, it's the exact opposite. All you're trying to do is just stay top of mind, let them know we're still here, we haven't gone under.

Martin Saenz:

You're working at different levels with government sales. You're not only doing those gentle touches with federal clients, you're doing that in conjunction with trying to find teaming partners that have immediate needs. I've found myself actually selling to government contractors that I was connecting with through associations. Your friend might find themselves training other federal contractors how to do a better job winning contracts. You never know where the road's going to lead you until you're driving 90 miles an hour.

Procurement Forecasts:

Chapter 10 is all about procurement forecasts, and a website called acquisition.gov. Just as usaspending.gov looks backward to see contracts that have already been let, acquisition.gov is forward looking, connecting you to procurement forecasts from various agencies.

Martin Saenz:

If you go to acquisition.gov right now, you will be looking at the procurement site for fiscal year 2018. You're going to see the name of the task that they're looking to procure, who the program manager is, what their telephone number is, how much they're looking to spend, what vehicle they're looking to procure it through, such as GSA Schedule, 8a, HUBZone, Service Disabled Veteran, Woman Owned

Small Business, etc. With that information, you can start pinpointing those individuals, agencies and program managers that you should be targeting going forward.

Your friend in the training business should look for training related items. They're not going to necessarily see their exact services on that procurement forecast. But, anytime they see something in the training area, then they're going to want to call that program manager, because that program manager probably also buys what your friend does. That person must go into your CRM system for later phone calls.

Capability Statement:

Chapter 12 talks about your capability statement, what folks in the commercial world might call a brochure. You stressed again that, like your marketing plan, like a lot of other things, you like to keep it short, keep it simple, keep it to one page. That is your recommendation?

Martin Saenz:

Yes, absolutely. Even if you have a multimillion-dollar company, you still need to keep your marketing plan and your capability statement short and simple, something that everyone can understand. The operations manual for my company is made up of mind maps. We use a company called XMind, and I do mind mapping, where I use pictures and graphics and just shorts texts, to describe different task areas. That's a lot easier for me to comprehend, and for a lot of other people to learn from, versus reading a hundred-page, dry operations manual. The objective is to have content presented in such a way that people can absorb it, retain it, and put it to good use. Simple is always best.

Proposal Generation System:

In Chapter 13 you present a spreadsheet that you created, which you call a Proposal Generation System. It plugs in a lot of information that you use repetitively to generate proposals much more quickly. I can see where it would be a time saving device if you are generating a lot of proposals. But my friend's training company, for example, probably doesn't send out more than three or four proposals a month, and that would be a busy month. How many proposals a month will you need to be generating, in order for your Proposal Generation System to become a time saver?

Martin Saenz:

At my company, during the July to September end of fiscal year period, we're finding nine to twelve items that we can respond to every day. I suspect that your friend's training company does not have a sophisticated sales system, that's working all the necessary angles, to deliver the maximum number of proposals that can be written per month.

End of Fiscal Year:

Chapter 14 is all about the end of the fiscal year. Because I've lived in DC all of my life, I've seen the news stories every year talking about agencies going crazy at the end of the fiscal year to spend all of the money that was allotted to them in their budget. If they don't spend it all in time they're not going to get the same amount or more in next year's budget. There's a big incentive for them to make sure they spend every last penny before the end of September.

In your course you emphasize to your employees that, during this period, it's all hands on deck. Vacations are canceled, forget about taking a sick day, we're going to be working seven days a week through August and September. For a smaller company, like my friend's training business, what sort of advice might you have for them? Would it be the same thing, that this is where you're really going to make your money for the year, so buckle down and start banging out some proposals?

Martin Saenz:

I would say you're going to be making your money in the down months, from October to February, because those should be the months when you're hungry and you're out there pounding the pavement. That's when you need to go see the OSDBU's, the small business officers, to go to industry days, to be calling teaming partners, to be looking through

FBO and continually calling on your directory of federal employees. There are several sites that actually will give you a white pages of sorts of federal employees, so you could be smiling and dialing all day long. If you're doing what you're supposed to be doing in the down months, then you're going to have a plentiful harvest when it comes to end of fiscal year.

If you don't put the work in during the rest of the year, you're creating a rollercoaster effect for yourself. You're leading from behind. If you wait for end of fiscal year to ramp up, well, why didn't you ramp up during the down time to ensure a better harvest come end of fiscal year. It's a 365-day game. Don't make it a short game. Don't be short-sighted and just hit it at end of fiscal year. Do all the work during the winter and put in the extra work during the summer. Then you'll become a large, profitable company.

Looking to Team?

Chapter 15 has to do with teaming. Personally, I worry about being a subcontractor for a person or a company that I'm not familiar with, and then not getting paid. I would also worry about subbing out work, that I'm responsible for the successful completion of, to a company or a person that I'm not familiar with. I'm not sure I can trust them to do what they're supposed to do. What are some red flags to look out for, green lights, and so forth, when considering teaming with another federal contractor?

Martin Saenz:

The same thing that the government contracting officer's doing, the same thing that potential teaming partners are doing – looking at your website to see if your marketing and branding present you as a competent professional – you should be doing that with anybody that you're considering associating yourself with. You are running in the social media circles, joining and participating with the government associations and becoming a thought leader in your area of expertise. What about this teaming partner you're considering? Are they known in those same circles as someone that's recognized as an ethical, upstanding person that really puts in the effort? You only want to be associating and aligning with people of that kind of character and personality.

This book focuses on selling to the federal government on a prime level. I have only done sub work on a few occasions, for Clark Construction, or some larger general contractors. 99% of the time I'm prime with the federal government. If you do choose to team with another contractor, you want to make sure that there's good chemistry between you two. You can learn a lot about the culture of any company by visiting their offices, spending time getting to know them and their employees personally. And, for goodness sake, always make sure you have good contractual terms laid out. Always have a good attorney drafting the team agreements.

Small Business Designations:

Chapter 16 discusses small business designations such as 8(a), Service Disabled Veteran, Woman Owned Small Business, etc. There is one thing that I'm not clear about; are these designations assigned solely by the Small Business Administration?

Martin Saenz:

The SBA does assign most of them, yes. For designations like Service Disabled Veteran Owned Small Business or Veteran Owned Small Business, the Department of Veteran Affairs has their own entity that deals with the certification process. I don't go into full detail in the book on this topic because it's not something a brand-new company should be focused on. It's more like a phase two for you as a new firm.

Sticking with the theme of keeping things simple, just start with the basics. Everything about your branding needs to look consistent. You need to be working social media every day, doing your competitive intelligence every day, FBO and procurement forecasts every day, going to industry days and attending association events on a regular basis. You have a lot of work to do starting out, so why don't you nail that down first? Become an expert at doing, and then expand your business later by getting your GSA Schedule, by finding out what designations you can apply for, etc.

Frank Felker:

Martin Saenz, thank you so much for joining me today.

Martin Saenz:

Thank you, Frank.